D1587448

K E F

ENGLISH CHURCHYARD MEMORIALS

For EDMUND, chauffeur and proof-reader

By the same author:

1993
Hallowed Ground
The Churchyards of Gloucestershire & the Cotswolds

1996
Hallowed Ground
The Churchyards of Wiltshire

1996
Cornwall's Churchyard Heritage

1998
Porch & Pew
Small Churches of the Cotswolds

ENGLISH
CHURCHYARD
MEMORIALS

TEMPUS

First published 2000

PUBLISHED IN THE UNITED KINGDOM BY:

Tempus Publishing Ltd
The Mill, Brimscombe Port
Stroud, Gloucestershire GL5 2QG

PUBLISHED IN THE UNITED STATES OF AMERICA BY:

Tempus Publishing Inc.
2 Cumberland Street
Charleston, SC 29401

Tempus books are available in France, Germany and Belgium
from the following addresses:

Tempus Publishing Group	Tempus Publishing Group	Tempus Publishing Group
21 Avenue de la République	Gustav-Adolf-Straße 3	Place de L'Alma 4/5
37300 Joué-lès-Tours	99084 Erfurt	1200 Brussels
FRANCE	GERMANY	BELGIUM

British Library Cataloguing in Publication Data.
A catalogue record for this book is available from the British Library.

ISBN 0 7524 1441 0

Typesetting and origination by Tempus Publishing.
PRINTED AND BOUND IN GREAT BRITAIN

Contents

ST. JAMES'S PALACE

For some years Hilary Lees has been campaigning to increase our awareness of the importance of the churchyard memorial as part of our historical and architectural heritage. Each one of the thousands of our churchyards up and down the country has a character of its own. Some are quiet, untrodden and overgrown, a haven for wildlife and flowers. Many have splendid examples of tombs and headstones bearing legends of dead infants, loyal servants and public and private figures. All of them are important as a reminder of our past and of the debt we owe our forebears. But the wonderful memorials which are to be found in many of them are often in a sad state of neglect and need careful attention and restoration if they are to be preserved for future generations.

I commend Hilary Lees' book and hope it will help to draw attention to this neglected aspect of our national heritage. I am sure that English Churchyard Memorials will be of interest not only to art historians, archaeologists and genealogists, but to all those who like to do what the antiquarian John Aubrey called 'grubbing in churchyards.'

Acknowledgements

I would like to thank all those people whose help and encouragement have made this book possible, especially:

Professor Bill Cotton

Robinette Deere

Joe Hemming

Francis Kelly

Jonathan MacKechnie-Jarvis, Gloucester DAC

Marian Ridd

Dr J. P. Toomey

Dorothy Wise

Tony and Mary Yoward

The author is greatly indebted to the Mark Fitch Fund for their generous assistance towards the costs of this project.

Hilary Lees 2000

The illustrations

Text figures

Colour illustrations

Front cover: Gadrooned chest at Elmore, Gloucs

All photographs by the author unless otherwise stated

1 God's Acre

For most people, the church is the physical and spiritual centre of the village. An elegant pinnacled tower, a distant spire glimpsed between tall trees, a tiny church come upon unexpectedly as you round a corner: each announces that this is a place, a community, a collection of people living together in this town or village. It occupies what is almost certainly the most ancient and most sacred site in the parish, and the God's Acre that surrounds it may be hundreds of years older than the church which now stands on it. Under its hallowed ground, mostly in unmarked graves, lie the remains of all those men, women and children who made this place into the community it is today. Many of them will have literally built the church or the surrounding houses, yet their only memorial is the green sward of the churchyard and perhaps a churchyard cross.

A churchyard memorial is more than a simple marker; it is a visible link between the living and the dead, and a means of establishing the identity of those we have loved and lost. It is also a reminder to those who come after of our own mortality and the frailty of human life. Long after memories have faded and families moved away, memorials continue to mirror the contemporary social scene. They are valuable records of changing social patterns, recording the lives and occupations of the people who lived and worked in that community at that time; many are excellent examples of vernacular art while others follow the changing whims of architectural design. Even when inscriptions too have worn away, the gravestone is a continuing reminder that this is a site of Christian burial on consecrated ground.

But a churchyard is more than just a burial ground; it provides the setting for the church, lending character and proportion to the building and enabling one to step back and see it in the context of its surroundings. In the same way the church is the backdrop for the churchyard; each will to some extent reflect the area in which it lies: the affluence of the sheep-wealth in the Cotswolds; the comfortable surroundings of the estate-churches and the simpler lives of the working villages. Each has a character all its own: it may be neglected and overgrown, the memorials tilted and broken, ivy eating into the inscriptions. Or it may be tidy and overmown until it is devoid of all character, the memorials moved to the boundary to make way for the all-consuming mower, or discarded altogether.

It is a corner of the parish that has remained almost unchanged for generations, a mine of information for historians, genealogists and archaeologists, and a legacy to the skills of our ancestors. What the antiquarian John Aubrey called 'grubbing in churchyardes' (sic) is for some a hobby or even a passion, for the art of the churchyard sculptor was and still is as much a part of our heritage as the church itself.

If there is one thing that a churchyard has that a cemetery lacks it is the feeling of antiquity, of the church and the churchyard being bound together in the history of the parish. In country towns and villages the materials used for the church, the churchyard boundary and the surrounding houses have often come from a local quarry; there is a harmony of colour and texture which is restful to the eye and adds to the character of the place. In some parts of the country, such as the Yorkshire Dales or Cornwall, it is not the architecture itself but the setting of the architecture that makes the impression; but every church and churchyard has an atmosphere of its own made up of its position, its materials, its gates and boundaries, as well as the memorials to the dead.

There are countless churchyards where the setting is perfection: Boxwell, a secluded hamlet on the western edge of the Cotswolds, down a hidden lane between box woods; the Eastleaches (Gloucs) where two churches face each other across the river Leach, spanned by John Keble's clapper bridge and a sea of daffodils in spring; Buscot (Oxon), where the churchyard is enclosed on three sides by the river; Gunwalloe (Cnwll) with its feet in the sea and its separate tower looking out stolidly over the bay; Hubberholme (N Yorks) favourite place of J B Priestley whose commemorative plaque says he found the church 'one of the smallest and pleasantest places in the world'. There are also those churchyards where you can stand with the church at your back and look outwards over stunning views; Saintbury (Gloucs), where the Vale of Evesham is laid out beneath your feet; East Peckham (Kent), or the hilltop churchyard of Shotley (Nthumb), where the Hopper mausoleum dominates the country for miles around **(Plate 1)**.

Many churchyards are approached through a lych gate, which, compared to the great age of many of our churches, will be relatively modern, most dating from the nineteenth and twentieth centuries. Many were built as war memorials or to commemorate individuals, and have been constructed with joinery of a mediaeval type. They are largely rural, and can present an attractive and unique approach to the churchyard or cemetery. The historical purpose of the lych gate — the name is derived from the Anglo-Saxon word *lich* for corpse — was to give the burial party an opportunity to rest while they waited for the priest, who was required by the Prayer Book of 1549, 'metyng the corpse at the church style' to begin the service from there. In many parts of the country the lych gate contains a coffin stone on which to rest the coffin, and seats for the bearers. In the middle ages those whose relatives were too poor to afford a coffin were laid on the coffin stone bound only in a sheet.

Coffin stones survive in a number of places including Pembury (Kent), Chilmark (Wilts), Kilkhampton (Cnwll) **(1)** and Sheepstor (Devon), where the gate is worked by a pulley mechanism. Duntisbourne Abbotts and North Cerney (Gloucs) have swivel gates designed to make the passage of the coffin easier, while Duntisbourne Rous has a diminutive lych gate opening on to a grassy path; at the other end is a rare scissor gate.

In the seventeenth century the priest's task was made more difficult because he had to ascertain that the body was wrapped in a shroud of wool; the law came into force in 1666 and was amended by statute in 1680 and 1687 to the effect that a penalty of £5 was incurred by those who did not comply. The law was not repealed until 1815, and must have provided a substantial boost to the coffers of the thriving wool trade.

Among the earliest lych gates are two in Kent, one to the old churchyard at Beckenham

*1 Coffin stone
and lych gate,
Kilkhampton,
Cornwall*

and another dated 1470 at Boughton Monchelsea. The mediaeval one at Anstey (Herts) was later converted to include the village lock-up, and in the same county the lych gate at Ashwell is also mediaeval, as is the one at the old churchyard at Beckenham (Kent). In Cornwall several lych gates have rooms above; Feock has two lych gates, which like Kenwyn and St Clement have slate hung upper rooms. A similar one at Long Compton (Warwks) is thatched. At Painswick (Gloucs) the lych gate was made out of the old timbers from the belfry, weathered to a silvery grey, with stone seats flanking the sides and bargeboards carved with bells. More recent is the extraordinary one at Great Bourton (Oxon) which incorporates the bell tower and was erected by a parishioner in 1883 in memory of his wife.

There are several ingenious devices to prevent animals getting into the churchyard. In Cornwall at St Just-in-Roseland, which must surely be the most stupendous churchyard view in the country, the lych gate has Cornish 'stiles' or cattle grids made of spaced stone slabs **(Plate 2)**. A number of Cornish churchyards such as Morwenstow and St Levan have slate stiles.

Where the churchyard gates are made of wrought iron they often merit more than a passing glance: Padstow (Cnwll) has two sets of elegant gates. At Melksham (Wilts) there is a beautiful pair of gates with eighteenth-century finials and acanthus leaves. At Morpeth (Nthumb) a complete entrance screen consists of an arcade of Romanesque arches with marble columns and cushioned capitals; scrolled railings fill the arches and the gates. In the same churchyard is a watch house, a reminder of the days when a watchman kept grave robbers at bay. At the simpler end of the scale is the horseshoe gate in the tiny parish of Clapton-on-the-Hill (Gloucs) with a similar one in the neighbouring parish of Farmington. It would be nice to think that the horseshoes had walked the Cotswold lanes before ending up in the gates.

Occasionally the churchyard wall has features of interest, like the bread prices in the wall at Wishford (Wilts), or the lock-up at Bromham in the same county which has a door from the churchyard as well as from the pavement. Buildings such as almshouses or parish rooms often form part of the boundary; others are less common, like the fourteenth century priest's house at Elkstone (Gloucs), the charnel house at Mere (Wilts), the old Guildhouse at Poundstock (Cnwll) or the dame school at Thursley (Surrey).

Surprisingly, nearly 40 churches in the country have detached towers or belfries. Cornwall has several; the slate tower at Gunwalloe with its pyramidal cap looks stolidly out to sea, while the one at Feock forms part of the boundary. The fourteenth-century belfry at Pembridge (Herefs) has a complex timber construction on masonry foundations.

The exterior of the church is as much part of the churchyard as the memorials themselves. It can be full of variety and interest, with parapets and pinnacles, gargoyles and grotesques, enriched doorways and ancient carvings. The church at Elkstone (Gloucs) has a Norman corbel table with figures from myth and legend; Steeple Ashton (Wilts) has enormous gargoyles and a huge sundial almost covering the face of the porch. The best collection of mediaeval grotesques must be on the church at Winchcombe (Gloucs) where there are about forty, said to be caricatures of the townspeople of the time and a reminder that mediaeval stonemasons were not without a sense of humour. Among other good collections are those at Adderbury (Oxon) Evercreech (Somset) and Coxwold (N Yorks). At Coates (Gloucs) is a gruesome anthropophagus — a man-eating monster — intended to demonstrate what will happen to those who fail to embrace the sacraments of the Church. Among the famous carvings on the church at Kilpeck (Herefs) is a sheela-na-gig, or pagan fertility carving; there is another at Oaksey (Wilts) and others at Church Stretton, Holdgate, Tugford (Shrops), Buncton (Sussex) and Whittlesford (Cambs). They show an old woman squatting in a grotesque, erotic posture; undoubtedly they originated on older buildings and because of their prevalence in Ireland are probably of Celtic origin.

In 'wool' country shears are sometimes found on the outside of churches as an indication that the church or part of it was built with 'wool' money. They can be seen on the towers of Cranham (Gloucs) and Minster (Cnwll) and in the window-splay at Seend (Wilts).

A great number of churches have wall plaques attached to outside walls, described by Kenneth Lindley[1] as 'parasitic growths upon other architectural forms' and not to be confused with headstones that have been removed from their original positions and attached to the wall. They are not restricted to the formal outline of the headstone and have often had some shelter from the weather. There is a charming one at Ampney Crucis (Gloucs) **(2)**, and others at Crudwell and Mere (Wilts). At Stoneleigh (Warwks) where the

2 *Wall plaque, Ampney
   Crucis. Gloucestershire
   1721*

churchyard is full of memorials to servants of the Leigh family of Stoneleigh Abbey, a large plaque is inset into an arch in the wall of the church:

To the memory of Humphry How, Porter to the Rt Hon[ble] the L[d] Leigh
Ob: 6 ffebr: An: D[o]ni 1688 Aetat 63.
Here Lyes a Faithful Friend unto the Poore
Who dealt Large Almes out of his Lord's store
Weepe Not Poore People Tho' Y[e] Servat's (sic) Dead
The Lorde Him Selfe Will Give You Dayly Breade
If markets Rife Raile Not Against Their Rates
The Price is Stil the same at Stonleigh gates.

Sundials on the south side of churches are common. Some Saxon sundials have survived, although their gnomons have long gone. There is a well-marked one at Oddington and a similar one at Saintbury (Gloucs) with deeply cut lines to indicate the times of important church services and lesser lines marking the hours. The fine Saxon dial over the south door at Daglingworth (Gloucs), a church famous for its Saxon carvings, has been protected by a later porch. A large number of churches have smaller dials, but they are not always easy to find. The late Saxon dial at Kirkdale (N Yorks) has an inscription detailing how the church was rebuilt from the ruins of the old one during the reign of Edward the Confessor and Tostig the Earl of Northumberland, brother of King Harold. This dates the church to approximately 1060. It also records the names of the two priests who made the sundial, Haward and Brand.

In the churchyard at Sutton Mandeville (Wilts) is a pillar sundial of 1685 with a ball finial and a clock face incised with Roman numerals. In Kent there is a small pillar sundial dated 1669 at Ightham and at Chilham is Inigo Jones' ornamental pedestal sundial. In slate areas, where they have weathered well, nearly every church has a seventeenth-century sundial. The one at Wenn (Cnwll) has a pun: 'Ye Know Not When'. At Lelant, where the churchyard overlooks the Hayle estuary, the sundial has an oddly-dressed skeleton holding an hourglass **(3)**. Over the church door at Eyam (Derbys) is an ambitious dial set on corbels which is dated 1775 and shows the time in various parts of the world.

Churchyards have their people, too: not only the armies of willing volunteers who cut the grass and carry dead flowers to the compost heap, but individuals whose work demonstrates a real devotion to their own patch of hallowed ground. The sexton at Kilkhampton (Cnwll) was extracted from the pub and led us unerringly across a vast churchyard to find the grave of an American who had asked as he died to be buried here. He lies facing the sea with no land between his grave and his distant homeland. Or the gardener at Coates (Gloucs) who leant on his rake to tell us in an accent as thick as custard that he had tended the churchyard, man and boy for fifty years.

In recent years the value of our churchyards as conservation areas has become increasingly recognised. They may be the only surviving unploughed, unsprayed meadowland in the parish, a haven for wildlife and rare plant species at a time when the surrounding farmland is becoming increasingly barren. In a churchyard of less than an acre there may be a hundred or more species of flowering plants, ferns, mosses and lichens; a living landscape for small mammals, birds, butterflies and moths. The flora and fauna in any one churchyard will be unique, the habitats depending on a number of variables, but nearly every churchyard will have something to offer, whether it is a carpet of bluebells in spring or an ancient creaking yew tree, almost as old as life itself. Different areas of grassland are managed for different habitats, which in the long run may well reduce the amount of work involved. The approach to the church and to recent burial areas is kept short, and the compost heap discreetly out of sight, essential to insects and hedgehogs; a larder and builders' merchants for birds, rich in food and nesting materials.

The Living Churchyard and Cemetery Project provides information and education on all aspects of wildlife conservation in churchyards. In his foreword to Francesca Greenoak's beautiful book, *God's Acre* Richard Mabey writes:

> At present, churchyards are regarded principally as resting places for the dead, where a respectful, sombre tidiness, clipped of all the excesses of nature, ought to prevail. That is an understandable feeling, but in the light of our growing sense of the interdependence of all life, a more hospitable attitude towards the rest of natural creation might perhaps be an apter response.

3   *Unusual sundial at Lelant,*
    Cornwall

To walk through an ancient churchyard is to step back in time; to absorb something of a place that has been sacred for hundreds, perhaps thousands of years. To feel that evocative emotion that is a mixture of quietude, nostalgia, and the vague reverence that we all have for death. To run your finger over carved cherubs' heads and decipher age-old names on leaning, lichen-covered stones. They tell us something of the nature and prosperity of the community; of the people who lived and worked in this parish: soldiers, farmers, wives, children, servants. Of how and when they died and who grieved for them. Many have inscriptions and epitaphs: sentimental, moral, humorous or merely factual, they give us an insight into social and family history. The churchyard memorial is itself a focal point for those who are bereaved, and its symbolism represents a statement of faith in the resurrection.

But most of all a churchyard should be a place for everyone, a suitable setting for the church, in keeping with the serious business of burial and an oasis of tranquillity: a place for rest and reflection among old friends.

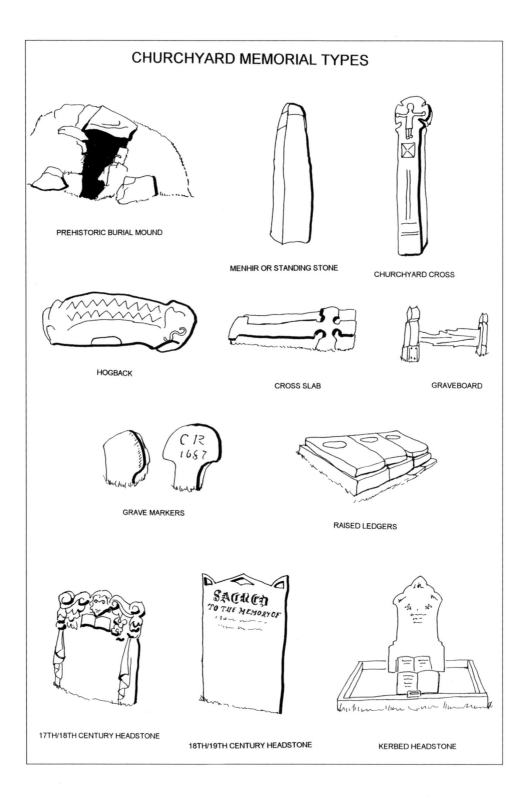

CHURCHYARD MEMORIAL TYPES

PREHISTORIC BURIAL MOUND

MENHIR OR STANDING STONE

CHURCHYARD CROSS

HOGBACK

CROSS SLAB

GRAVEBOARD

GRAVE MARKERS

RAISED LEDGERS

17TH/18TH CENTURY HEADSTONE

18TH/19TH CENTURY HEADSTONE

KERBED HEADSTONE

BODY STONES

CHEST TOMB

TABLE TOMB

BALE TOMB

COTSWOLD TOMB

PEDESTAL TOMB

MAUSOLEUM

GREEK REVIVAL TOMB

MONUMENT

MODERN MARITIME MONUMENT

2 The history of the churchyard

Since prehistoric times it has been customary to mark the place of burial as a sign of respect for the dead and a focal point for the grief of the bereaved. Thousands of years before Christianity or the Roman invasion of England, the burial of the dead and the rituals associated with it were an important part of the life and death of our ancestors. Stonehenge and nearby Avebury are among the most important tomb-complexes of Europe; they demonstrate the significance attached by early man to burials close to monuments of religious, if pagan significance, which led ultimately to the Christian custom of burying the dead in or near buildings of religious importance.

Prehistoric man considered a tomb to be a house for the dead, and the grave goods, or artefacts, which were interred with the corpse indicated a religious or mystical belief in an afterlife. Many of the earliest and most impressive stone monuments were simply a horizontal slab placed across two uprights demonstrated so effectively by the sheer magnitude of Stonehenge. On a lesser scale but no less impressive are the portal dolmens such as Trevethy Quoit at St Cleer in Cornwall and the Rollright stones in the Oxfordshire Cotswolds. These smaller megalithic survivals have a starkness about them, situated as they are in a high, barren landscape.

The long barrows of the Neolithic Age were communal chambered tombs divided into sections by large vertical stones capped with horizontal slabs. They were designed for successive burials, the prehistoric equivalent of the family vault of today, and when complete were covered with earth. Belas Knapp long barrow at Sudeley (Gloucs) was built in about 3000 BC and has four burial chambers, a horned forecourt and side entrances. It may have been used as an earlier burial site before the barrow was built.

The characteristic burial mound of the later Neolithic and early Bronze Age is the round barrow, which may have covered only a single interment in a stone chamber or cist. In 1900 a cemetery of stone cist graves was discovered at Harlyn Bay (Cnwll) containing grave goods of Mediterranean origin. At Aylesford (Kent) an Iron Age cemetery was excavated close to the churchyard.

The custom of burial beneath tumuli continued until the Anglo-Saxon period, and the remains of ancient burial mounds can often be seen in modern churchyards. At Ogbourne St Andrew (Wilts) there is a large bowl barrow in the churchyard in which a pagan Saxon burial was found, and at Tilshead in the same county a number of skeletons, believed to be those of invading Danes, were found buried without coffins in hollowed-out chalk.

Under Roman law the burial of the dead over the age of 40 days was forbidden within the town defences. Until the second century cremation was the customary form of disposal, but from the third century onwards burials took place in rectangular cemeteries outside the city boundaries. The dead were placed in wooden coffins, although the wealthy and important had covered stone coffins. In the churchyard at South Cerney (Gloucs) is an enormous Saxon coffin and two carved lids, which were found on a Saxon burial site and brought to their present position. A similar monolithic coffin has survived in the churchyard at Low Dinsdale (Dur).

Christianity was established in Britain by the fourth century, although many converts clung to their pagan beliefs. The early converts during the Roman occupation seem to have been confined to urban areas and to the wealthy in their villas, as can be seen from the number of Christian symbols, notably the Chi-Rho monogram found on the sites of Roman villas such as Hinton St Mary and Frampton (Dorset), Lullingstone (Kent) and Chedworth (Gloucs). The famous word-square or cryptogram found at Cirencester (Gloucs) in 1868, together with other examples found in the Roman world, are now considered to be of Christian significance.

$$R \; O \; T \; A \; S$$
$$O \; P \; E \; R \; A$$
$$T \; E \; N \; E \; T$$
$$A \; R \; E \; P \; O$$
$$S \; A \; T \; O \; R$$

Translated, it means: 'The sower Arepo holds the wheel carefully'.

In Wales and the west, Celtic Christianity developed independently from the rest of Britain under the influence of Irish saints such as Saint Patrick, and the multitude of Cornish saints whose names can still be found in the unusual dedications of the churches of Cornwall.

Because of their pagan origins many churchyards are much older than even the earliest wooden churches that stood on them. Many stand on known prehistoric sites, such as Avebury (Wilts), Breedon-on-the-Hill (Leics) and Knowlton (Dorset). Circular churchyards such as Ozleworth (Gloucs), Rudston (E York) and Wirksworth (Derbys), St Buryan and Lanivet (Cnwll) in particular are known to be ancient pagan sites. A number of sites have produced evidence of a previous use: Widford (Oxon) and Woodchester (Gloucs) are both on the sites of Roman villas; at Tintagel (Cnwll) archaeologists have unearthed a pre-Norman stone church and ample evidence of burials from the early Christian to the post mediaeval period.

In 563 Columba came to Iona to begin the conversion of England in the north. He died there in 597, the same year that Pope Gregory '... sent the servant of God, Augustine and with him several other monks, who feared the Lord, to preach the word of God to the English nation'.[1] The efficient planning of the Conversion was to have far-reaching effects on the subsequent development of the church and its ultimate organisation over ensuing centuries. Priests travelled out from monastic houses or minsters and established early Christian sites within previously pagan boundaries, which were purified and dedicated to the Christian faith. In this way the undecided among the converts were more likely to accept the new faith at a place they already considered to be sacred; in fact many continued to venerate standing stones, thus as it were, keeping their options open. So effective was this policy in recruiting converts that in 601 Pope Gregory sent instructions to his missionaries that pagan temples were not to be destroyed, but were to be converted to the new faith. Where the population were still venerating standing stones the missionaries compromised by inscribing them with a cross or a sun symbol; often the folklore associated with standing stones persisted for centuries.

In the churchyard at Braunston (Leics) is a 1.2m high carved stone which would appear to be a pagan fertility figure, and may have been an object of worship there before the arrival of Christianity.

The priest would first have set up a stone or wooden cross with a makeshift altar to the north of it under some form of cover, until such time as a more permanent building was erected. It was a natural progression from there to building some sort of shelter for the congregation, the origin of the belief that lasted for centuries, although not formalised until the thirteenth century, that the nave was the responsibility of the congregation and the chancel was the property of the priest. Here he would celebrate Mass, baptise converts and preach. Initially, when the priest died he would have been buried in the churchyard beneath his own cross, and gradually lay members of the congregation were allowed to be buried in the same place, close to their spiritual leader. Later, when the church building was established, the priest and ultimately the laity were buried within the church, the priest usually close to the altar, the congregation under the nave.

Bede, describing the situation following the Synod of Whitby in 664, wrote:

> ... so that wheresoever any clergyman or monk happened to come, he was joyfully received by all persons, as God's servant; and if they chanced to meet him upon the way, they ran to him, and bowing, were glad to be signed with his hand, or blessed with his mouth.[2]

It was in 752 that St Cuthbert was granted permission by the Pope to establish churchyards around churches, the four cardinal points being marked with crosses. It was not until the tenth century that the practice of enclosing churchyards was introduced, the origin of the name 'God's Acre', which created a defined area for the burial of the dead. All early burials took place on the south side of the church, possibly a relic of the pagan worship of the sun-god. The north side was deemed to be the domain of the devil and was viewed with fear and superstition; it was reserved for undesirables such as unbaptised infants, criminals and suicides. Many churches still have a north door which would have been opened during the baptism service to allow the evil spirits to escape. On the north side of the church at Grade (Cnwll) is a slate ledger that once covered a chest-tomb nearby. The curious epitaph may indicate that this was the first burial on the north side: [3]

> Here lyeth the body of Hugh Mason gentleman, who departed this life in the fear of God the third day of December 1671 at the age of 65.
> Why here? Why not? 'Tis all one ground
> And here none will my dust confound
> My Saviour lay where no one did
> Why not a member as his head?
> No quire to sing, no bells to ring?

Why Sirs! Thus buried was my King!
I grudge the fashion of this day
To fat the church and starve the lay
Though nothing of me now be seene
I hope my name and bed is greene.

Although pagan beliefs and practices were not far below the surface the churchyard became recognised as an area of sanctuary to which people could flee when danger threatened. A relic of a pagan ritual which has survived to this day is the ceremony of 'Clypping the Church' which is still held annually Wirksworth (Derbys) and at Painswick (Gloucs), where the children of the parish joins hands and dance round the church in a symbolic gesture of embracement.

The great explosion of church building which followed the Norman Conquest would have done much to reinforce the importance of the church and its surroundings in the minds of the people. Burials inside churches became customary from the twelfth century and throughout the Middle Ages the wealthy had elaborate memorials erected inside the church. The poor were buried in unmarked graves in the churchyard, in a simple shroud and without a coffin. G H Cook[4] describes them rather neatly as the 'uncoffined dead'. The body would be laid on its back with the head to the east on an east/west alignment, a relic of pagan worship of the sun-god. Only a priest would be brought to the service and interred 'versus altare', ie facing his congregation, a practice which continues today. The burials started at one end of the churchyard and when the burial ground was full they would go back to the beginning and start again. Eventually there would be several layers of bones in shallow graves and it became necessary to remove some of them to a crypt or charnel house in the church. Similarly if there were alterations or extensions to the church, excavated remains would have to be removed. Few charnel houses survive in their original form, but the one at Rothwell (Nhants) still has the bones neatly stacked, and there is another at Hythe (Kent). G H Cook describes several 'bone-holes,' including those at Westbury-on-Trym (Bristol) and Cirencester (Gloucs) but it is doubtful how many now survive; after the Reformation many were taken over for use as family vaults.

Kenneth Lindley[5] estimated that a small twelfth-century churchyard with only six burials a year would by now contain some 4,800 bodies. In several ancient churchyards there is such an accumulation that the ground has been raised by several feet, and it has been necessary to dig a channel round the church for drainage purposes. In the churchyard at Kilpeck (Herefs) the level of the ground has risen to the top of the churchyard wall; and at Thurlow (Suffk) the outline of a row of burials can actually be seen through the turf.

The Synod of Exeter in 1287 directed that parish priests should forbid the use of churchyards for unseemly activities, but this appears to have had little effect, perhaps because the parish priest was unwilling to relinquish this source of income. Especially on Feast Days the mediaeval churchyard became the centre of village life in much the same way as the village hall of today. Fairs and markets were held with livestock being bought and sold; musicians played, travelling pedlars sold their wares and competitions in archery and other sports were held, all of which helped augment the priest's income. In the church porch at Oddington (Gloucs) there are grooves on the stone bench in the porch said to have been made by archers sharpening their arrows. The priest also had the right to graze the garth, and willow wands were often placed over graves to protect them from desecration, a practice known as 'brambling'. In Arthur Hughes' painting *'Home from the Sea*, of an orphaned sailor boy weeping in Chingford (Gtr. London) churchyard, a brambled grave is clearly visible. Later decorative forms in cast iron can be seen at Sutton Veny (Wilts) and Henham (Essex).

'Church Ales' were held on feast days to finance improvements to the church and to raise money for the poor; these were so successful that a number of parishes built a church house for their church ales, and many of these survive today.

Many instances of inappropriate behaviour in both church and churchyard were recorded by the church authorities. At Grantham (Lincs) in 1469 a tanner, Thomas Wortley, was ordered to read a confession in the market place. His offence was that:

> ... the said Thomas Wortley in the nyghte tyme smote violently on Edward Syngar, a minister of the churche of Grantham whereby the said churcheyard was polluted and of the administration all sacramentalles suspended, to the grete displeasure of God, contempt to our modern Holy Churche and grete noyance and offense to all this paryshe ....[5]

The church porch was considered to be the place for serious business, for the taking of oaths and the settling of disputes. Many porches still have an image niche in front of which solemn vows were sworn. In 1624 John Evelyn recalls having lessons in the porch at Malmesbury (Wilts), and at Northleach (Gloucs) the priest lived in the room above the porch.

A number of parishes still have remnants of a burial path, by which the dead were brought to the church on the parish bier from the outlying hamlets for the burial service. In the parish of Bisley (Gloucs) the Pope removed the burial rites from the parish as a penalty, after the parish priest fell into the churchyard well and drowned; for two years the villagers had to carry their dead to Bibury for burial. The ancient well was then filled in and used as a Poor Souls' light.

Churchyard history also has its darker side. During the Civil War a battle was fought in the churchyard at Alton (Hants) and prisoners were held in a number of Gloucestershire churchyards. At Burford (Oxon) men were executed in the churchyard when Cromwell's soldiers put down a Levellers' rising in 1649. Ripley (N Yorks) and Didbrook (Gloucs) have bullet holes in the church doors.

From the beginning of the seventeenth century churchyard memorials became commonplace as space ran out inside the churches and the rising middle classes wanted permanent reminders of their increasing affluence. Many of them can only be described as ostentatious symbols of family wealth and pride. In the country churchyard the yeoman (farmer) outnumbers landowners and merchants. Wealthy and influential families continued to be buried inside the church; most older churches are honeycombed under

4 Plaque to William Tasker
   'who would rather be a
   doore-keeper,' Corsham.
   Wilts, 1684

the floor with intramural burials.

On the outside wall of the church at Linkinhorne (Cnwll) is a stone commemorating the deaths of Catherine Nicholls and Joan Mullins who died in 1742 and 1744 respectively. The stone is carved with a skeleton, an arrow and a spade, and is signed by Daniel Gumb, an eccentric stonemason who lived with his wife and children in a lonely cottage near the Cheesewring. The epitaph reflects the feelings of those buried outside the church:

> Here we lye without the wall
> Twas full within they made a brawl
> Here we lye no rent to pay
> Yet we lye so warm as they.

There are similar ones at Kingsbridge (Devon) and Corsham (Wilts), where William Tasker, who died in 1684 'would rather be a doore keeper to the house of his God than dwell in the tents of wickedness' **(4)**. Between the seventeenth and the nineteenth centuries there was a distinct change in attitude towards the disposal of the dead. At the time when the wealthy had memorials inside the church and the poor were buried in the churchyard there seemed to be no feeling of respect for the burial site and no sense of ownership of the grave among family members. It was not uncommon for the remains to be disturbed or removed, or for bones to lie about in the churchyard as in Hogarth's contemporary engraving of 'The Idle Prentice at Play in the Churchyard During Divine Service'. In most cases the earliest churchyard memorials were small, insignificant stones inscribed only with initials and a date; there was little attempt to publicise the name or occupation of the deceased. The living viewed death as the transition between this world and the next and seem to have had few emotional concerns about the physical remains.

During the course of the eighteenth century and the tremendous increase in the numbers of churchyard memorials all this was to change, due largely to the increased affluence of the new merchant classes, yeoman farmers and clothiers. The burial site began to be seen as a piece of family property to be identified and visited as such. Tombs were erected in family groups and often one tomb would be used for subsequent burials; any removal of remains would have been unthinkable.

By the end of the eighteenth century the family grave was almost a status symbol. The attitudes of the living towards the dead were changing as the bereaved related more closely to the deceased: grief was more public and visiting the grave of the departed was a weekly ritual that was to continue until our own time. Inscriptions became more emotional and flowery, especially those relating to children, as the memorial became a tangible link between the living and the dead. This attitude was encouraged by the so-called graveyard poets, who wrote melancholy, reflective works, often set in churchyards, on the theme of human mortality. The best known was Thomas Gray whose *Elegy Written in a Country Church-Yard*, composed in 1751. On a similar theme was James Hervey's *Meditations Among the Tombs*, an enormously lengthy contemplative prose poem. Hervey (1714-58) was a prominent early Methodist.

The nineteenth century and the rise of the cemetery brought something approaching equality to the business of burial. Now the high-born and the humble could lie side by side in peace; burial had become the profitable business of the funeral parlour in orderly and undisturbed dignity.

The finest period of churchyard architecture is the 150 years from 1700, when the height of the Cotswold 'wool' trade is so richly reflected in churchyards such as Painswick (Gloucs).

The nineteenth century and the Industrial Revolution, with its massive migration of the population into towns and cities, produced a serious problem of overcrowding in city churchyards. London churchyards had become so foul that gravediggers were said to have been permanently drunk in order to endure the work. At about the same time medical schools were being established and with the demand for bodies for dissection grave-robbing became a profitable business and fear of the 'resurrection-men' became a widespread concern. As much as £20 was said to be the going price for a 'good, clean corpse.' To deter would-be thieves, heavy stones called 'body-snatcher' stones were placed on newly-dug graves; a body-snatcher stone survives in the Unitarian graveyard at Frenchay (Bristol).

With city churchyards becoming increasingly foul and unhygienic the Burial Act of 1832 was passed to allow cemeteries to be set up; they were established by local authorities in the same way as drainage and water services to accommodate the urgent need created by the rapid increase in population. The modern cemetery, with its regimented rows of foreign stones and polished marble, is the result of improvements in transport and the rise of the monumental mason. They have little of the character of a churchyard: there are few mature trees and little local stone, encrusted with lichens and mosses and mellowing gradually over the years.

The more recent practice of cremation, which was only legalised in 1884, has brought the modern fashion for small memorial plaques which line the path or form a Garden of Remembrance.

The Nonconformist Churchyard

The Nonconformist burial ground is one of the commonest and one of the most overlooked, yet at their height the total of Baptist, Congregational, Methodist and Quaker graveyards must have totalled more than those of the established Church. Many have survived, although often the chapels have long since been acquired for other purposes. One of the smallest must be the tiny churchyard attached to the now disused Congregational church at Edge (Gloucs). Two memorials stand in an area no bigger than a village duckpond; one of them commemorates William James Steele who died in 1967 and was the last preacher at the chapel.

In the seventeenth and eighteenth centuries the Quakers saw the development of churchyard monuments as arrogant and ostentatious. They described churchyards as 'steeple-house yards'; their own burial grounds usually surrounded their meeting houses and had no monuments. The picturesque thatched Quaker meeting house at Come-To-Good (Cnwll) has stabling for the horses and only smooth green turf covering the burial ground. In later years the rules were relaxed slightly; the Quaker burial ground at Street (Somset) has small uniform headstones bearing only the initials and date of death of the deceased.

Other denominations seem to have been less austere, and many Baptist and Unitarian graveyards are no more restrictive than parish churchyards and often better cared for. The Baptist chapel yard at New Mill (Herts) has one of the best Nonconformist collections of memorials, many featuring religious symbolism which would have horrified the early Quakers. In the hamlet of Cote, near Bampton (Oxon) are some finely carved headstones in front of the old chapel (5).

The Nonconformists welcomed the development of cemeteries as being independent of the Church of England; the seventeenth-century burial ground at Bunhill Fields in the City of London was the first to be set up outside the Establishment. In the cemetery at Mere (Wilts) an area has been set aside for Quaker burials, all with small identical headstones.

The most interesting Nonconformist burial is at Newby (Cumb) where a small stone-walled and long-abandoned Quaker burial ground occupies the middle of a field. In one corner the top of a chest tomb has been set on end inside a stone-built shelter (6). The inscription records the death of Thomas Lawson in 1691, aged 61. He was said to be the most noted herbalist of his time, with a number of plants being first described by him and one, *Hieracium Lawsonii*, named after him.

5   Carved headstones at Cote, Oxfordshire

Folklore

In the redundant churchyard of Cooling St James (Kent) is a row of children's graves that are said to have been the inspiration for the opening pages of Dickens' *Great Expectations*. The opening scene describes the churchyard as a 'bleak place' in which the unfortunate Pip was set upon by the convict Magwitch. He watched him lumber off 'as if he were eluding the hands of the dead people, stretching up cautiously out of their graves, to get a twist upon his ankle and pull him in.' A churchyard which is a pleasant and restful place by day can feel completely different at night, as William Shakespeare described so graphically in *Hamlet*:

> 'Tis now the very witching time of night,
> When churchyards yawn, and hell itself breathes out
> Contagion to the world.

For many people a churchyard is still a place that arouses vague feelings of unease, of supernatural events and ghosts wandering among the graves. To our ancestors death was the ultimate mystery, wrapped in rituals and superstitions that were a relic of pagan beliefs. In the Middle Ages a highly superstitious congregation believed that the Devil, although excluded from the church itself, still existed in the churchyard, particularly in the shadow of the north side. Grotesque figures on the outside of the church were meant to keep evil spirits at bay; stones were placed over the eyes of the dead because it was believed that evil spirits escaped through the eye sockets.

Folklore has perpetuated some of these superstitions to the present day: chariots are

6 *Memorial to*
   Thomas Lawson,
   1691 at Newby,
   Cumbria

said to hurtle along the churchyard wall at Stratton St Margaret (Wilts). At Uley (Gloucs) there is a legend about a veteran of the Peninsular Wars who could remember a skeleton being found near his home. It was believed to be that of a pedlar who had disappeared some time before and was presumed to have been murdered. The skeleton was laid in the church porch on Sundays; the belief was that if the man who murdered him came by, the skeleton would bleed.

At St Levan (Cnwll) is a large rock known as St Levan's stone; legend has it that St Levan, thought to have been a sixth- or seventh-century Celt, lived on a diet of one fresh fish a day. He used to rest on the rock when tired from fishing, and one day when he was an old man he took his rod and struck the rock, which broke in two. He prayed over the stone and made the prophecy:

> When with panniers astride
> a pack horse can ride
> through St Levan's stone,
> the world will be done.

On the island of Portland (Dorset) halfway down the cliff behind Pennsylvania Castle is the ruined church of St Andrew, now little more than an outline on the ground and a single chancel arch. Nearby are a few memorials and among them two chest tombs carved with skulls and crossbones. Legend has it that these are the graves of smugglers and pirates, and certainly that would fit in with the atmosphere of this forgotten corner. According to folklore in several places, smugglers would use chest tombs to conceal their booty, in the hope that superstition would prevent the authorities disturbing or searching the graves.

Since pagan times evergreens and in particular yew trees have been associated with churchyard folklore and rituals. Because it lives to a great age the yew is seen as a symbol of immortality, the fountain of ancient wisdom, older than any other living thing and the keeper of the secret of life itself. In the middle ages branches of yew were laid on the coffin or shroud to ward off evil spirits and as a symbol of immortality; their red cupped berries were regarded as drops of blood.

There are a number of very ancient yews such as the one at Fortinghall (P&K) which is estimated to be 5,000 years old and which pre-dates Christianity. Another at Tandridge (Surrey) was mature when the Saxons built the church, because they incorporated stone vaulting into the foundations to accommodate the roots of the tree. There is one theory that early churches were built on sites already made sacred by the pagan belief of the mystical powers of the yew tree.

In the Middle Ages the Green Man, or Jack-in-the-Green, symbol of rebirth and the immortality of nature, was often carved high in the roofs of churches and cathedrals. Occasionally he appears on churchyard memorials; a logical, if pagan, representation of resurrection.

SALTASH 1747

3 The churchyard cross

The Christian churchyard cross has its origins in the pagan monolith or standing stone. The worship of stones may have developed from man's first use of them for commemoration and the belief among pagan worshippers that they were the spiritual residences of the dead. The most spectacular survival is the Bronze Age monolith at Rudston, (E. Yorks).[1] It is the largest standing stone in Britain, at 8m high, 1.75 m wide and one metre thick at the base. It is estimated to weigh about twenty-six tons. It stands at the centre of a number of important archaeological sites in the area and only a couple of metres from the more recent church, an interesting example of a site of pagan significance which was later converted to Christianity. The earliest monuments marked with a cross have been found in Scotland, Wales and Cornwall.

Perhaps the earliest identified memorial is the third-century Goreus stone outside the church door at Yealmpton (Devon). It is a narrow, flat granite monolith standing 1.8m high with the name GOREUS roughly carved on the east face. It is thought to commemorate an early British chieftain. Another at Stowford (Devon) now barely legible, has a vertical inscription which reads GURGLES, GUNGLEI, GOMGEL, GUNGLEL.

Wales and the areas where Celtic traditions survived are in some respects almost another country; they were little affected by the Romans, they had their own language and Celtic traditions and were geographically remote.

MYLOR
IN THE CHURCHYARD

A drawing estimating the full height of Mylor cross (Langdon, Old Cornish Crosses)

Mylor Cross, Cornwall

31

After the retreat of the Romans in the middle of the fifth century the development of the churchyard cross was influenced by a combination of factors: the culture and stability of invading forces, their religious affiliation and the materials available. Into the north and north-east came the Danish and Norse influence; into the south-east came the Mediterranean influence, while the Celtic Christians retreated to the west.

In Cornwall are a number of inscribed stones which were probably early grave markers converted with a Christian emblem. The Chi-Rho monogram, made up of the letters XP, the first two letters of the Greek word for Christ, is on the gable of the church porch at Phillack, with others inside the churches at St Just-in-Penwith and Lanteglos-by-Fowey. Inscribed stones dating from the fifth to the seventh centuries would have commemorated figures of great importance, and can be found at St Hilary and Phillack. There are others at Gulval, Lanteglos-by-Camelford and South Hill. In the churchyard at Lewannick, with another inside the church, is a stone inscribed with Ogham lettering, a curious script which originated in southern Ireland and is made up of unconnected vertical lines. It can be dated fairly accurately to the late fifth or early sixth century. There are other Ogham stones at St Clement and St Kew.

In the churchyard at Lanteglos-by-Camelford is a pillar stone with a Saxon inscription and nearby an early Celtic cross with stumpy projecting arms. On the north side of the church is the modern burial ground with black marble memorials, an interesting juxtaposition of the old and the new.

The churchyard cross is by far the most common surviving Anglo-Saxon monument, although untold numbers will have been lost or destroyed. Fragments are often found built into churches as lintels, used in the foundations of a later building or even built into the churchyard wall. Crosses, whether whole or fragmented, can reliably be said to have had their origins close to where they are found, being heavy and less portable than other artefacts such as jewellery or coins.

The early Christian missionaries would have carried wooden crosses or staffs which were set up as preaching crosses and symbols of the sanctity of consecrated ground. They may even have become the marker for the priest's own burial site, creating a religious significance for his followers and a desire for them to be buried close to their spiritual leader. As the centres of religion became established they would have been replaced by stone crosses until by the Reformation every churchyard would have at least one stone cross.

A number of surviving Anglo-Saxon crosses have been taken inside for safe keeping, including those at Hexham (Nthumb), Otley (N Yorks) and the one *c.*790 from Easby (W Yorks) which is in the Victoria and Albert Museum, although a plaster replica stands in the church. Of those still in their original churchyard positions and among the most important are those at Ruthwell (D & G), Bewcastle, Gosforth and Irton (all Cumb) and Masham (N Yorks) **(7)**. The remote churchyard at Bewcastle is deceptively peaceful, with lichened headstones round the feet of the cross, but this was once the site of a Roman fort on Hadrian's Wall, and must have seen plenty of conflict between the Romans and the 'Barbarians.' The cross, which dates from the seventh or early eighth century, stands 4.3m tall, is made of sandstone and is still in its original position. It is carved with vine scrolls and interlaced knotwork, carved figures and birds, as well as Runic inscriptions and is

*7 Anglo-Saxon cross shaft,
Masham, N Yorks*

thought to commemorate King Alcfrith. It would originally have carried a free-armed Anglian cross, and it is said that in the seventeenth century the head was sent to the antiquary William Camden for examination and never returned. It is one of the most impressive survivals from the early days of Christianity; there was no precedent for artistic work of this quality, and it seems likely that the skilled craftsmen who were brought from the Mediterranean to work on the monasteries imported the iconography **(8) (Plate 3)**.

The slender, tapered cross at Gosforth (Cumb) dating from the tenth century and still in its original socket-stone, is cut from a single stone with a beautifully proportioned wheelhead cross and is 4.2m high. It is sandstone, decorated with a mixture of Scandinavian and Christian mythology, indicating the influence of Norse settlers from Ireland and the Isle of Man. It bears a carving of the Crucifixion in which Christ is not nailed to the Cross, and the soldier with the spear is accompanied by a pigtailed female figure, possibly that of a Valkyrie, who in Norse mythology welcomed heroes to Valhalla, the great hall of Odin.

In the churchyard at Irton (Cumb), south of Gosforth the smaller cross dates from the ninth century. It is decorated with interlace and the cross has expanded arms and nailhead ornament, The round shaft in the churchyard at Masham (N Yorks) dates from the ninth

8   Detail of the Bewcastle cross, Cumbria

9   Inscribed cross figure of Christ, Sancreed, Cornwall

century and is carved with figures and animals. At Bakewell (Derbys) where the church is dramatically situated on a hill above the town, the ninth-century shaft is decorated with human figures as well as animals. Another from the same date at Eyam (Derbys) retains its head. In the beautiful setting of the church at Ilam Park (Staffs) are two tenth-century cross shafts decorated with interlace; unfortunately the tops of both are badly weathered.

Cornwall has the largest number of crosses, many of which would have had pre-Christian significance and been subsequently consecrated to the Christian faith. Most of the earliest crosses are of the type known as Celtic, with a round head or with square arms linked by a circular ring, and originated in Ireland and the Western Isles. A large number are not in churchyards: wayside crosses marked the pilgrim routes in what was then a wild and desolate area. There is an old tradition which says that the richer pilgrims would leave alms by the wayside crosses for the poorer pilgrims who followed. In 1447 the Rector of

Creed (Cnwll) left a bequest requiring that wayside crosses should be erected 'where dead bodies rested on their way to burial, so that prayers may be made and the bearers take some rest'.

In Cornwall one can see the wheelhead cross in every shape and form, from the early cross with short projecting arms like a child's drawing at Lanteglos-by-Camelford to the inscribed crosses complete with the figure of Christ at Sancreed **(9)** and the holed cross at Phillack, which date from the tenth century or later. These later ones are easier to date, as other documentation of the same period contains similar ornament.

Cornish churchyards crosses — and there are hundreds, with the greater number in the west and frequently two or more in one churchyard — are not the intricately-carved high crosses of the north. These humbler cousins are of granite, a material which does not lend itself to delicate carving, but has a solidity and rough texture that is somehow reassuring to the eye, representing as it does a continuity of faith as enduring as the Cornish themselves. One of the earliest is the sixth-century four-holed cross head at Wendron.

From the eighth to the twelfth century the figure of Christ was shown alive, dressed in a tunic, the limbs extended along three arms of the cross, the head erect on the fourth. Arthur G Langdon in his definitive book *Old Cornish Crosses* describes the representations of Christ as 'of the rudest and most grotesque description, being executed in low relief, rarely projecting more than an inch'. He particularly draws attention to the cross at St Levan which also has the figure of Christ as 'most elegant and well-proportioned' and the beautiful cross shaft with interlace ornament at St Neot as 'the best example of interlaced work in Cornwall.'

The Celtic cross at Mylor is probably the oldest Celtic cross in England and may have originated as a pre-Christian monolith. With seven feet of its total height of seventeen in the ground it is certainly the tallest. But the finest cross in the county must be the four-holed cross at Cardinham **(Plate 4)** which has knotwork on the front face and interlace on the back, with the shaft divided into three panels, the top one with an inscription and the others with plaitwork. It has been dated at about 800 AD; by the gate in the same churchyard is another, dated at 900 AD which is mounted on an inscribed stone from the Roman occupation.

Just inside the eighteenth-century wrought iron gates at Padstow is an enormous cross-base and part of a shaft, dug up in the churchyard. Langdon says that from the size of it, it would have been the largest cross in Cornwall. Local folklore has it that if anyone should sit on it they would hear the roar of the Devil, incarcerated beneath.

The mediaeval cross

Throughout the Middle Ages, when the wealthy were buried inside the church, the rest of the population were buried in the churchyard in unmarked graves. The churchyard cross is often the only memorial to the hundreds of people whose lives were centred on the church and whose remains are interred beside it. It played an important part in the processional rituals of the church, being used as a preaching station on days of prayer and thanksgiving such as Palm Sunday.

The mediaeval churchyard cross usually had a large square or rectangular base of individual stones built up to three or four steps. Occasionally the side panels would be decorated with quatrefoils, as at Didmarton (Gloucs). Above this the socket stone, standing taller than the steps below, might also have decoration and chamfered or panelled faces. At Mileham (Norfk) a fifteenth-century cross with four narrow niches in the head stands on a quatrefoiled chest tomb base.

The shaft was usually square in cross-section, tapering towards the top, and with chamfered edges ending in a stop. Between the shaft and the head there may be a capital or a roll, or the base of the head may be corbelled out from the shaft. The mediaeval cross at Bitterley (Shrops) has a hole through the centre of the shaft, the purpose of which is uncertain, but perhaps connected with some religious ritual.

A beautiful example of a complete fourteenth-century cross is the one at St Mary's, Cricklade (Wilts), where the four-sided lantern head has its original sculpture complete, and rests on corbel heads. At Ampney Crucis (Gloucs) the gabled cross head was found walled up inside the church, presumably to hide it from the iconoclasts. The head has a crucifixion on one face and the Virgin on the other, and on one of the sides a man in armour of *c.*1415. Among other mediaeval crosses in good condition are those at Chewton Mendip and Spaxton (Somset), Higham Ferrars (Hants), Walcot (Lincs) and Dorchester (Oxon). In Cornwall there are lantern crosses at Lanteglos-by-Fowey and Mawgan-in-Pydar.

Just outside the church door at Ripley (N Yorks) is a rare, if not unique, example of the base and stump of a 'weeping cross', with eight deeply-carved recesses where penitents would kneel in prayer. It is estimated to be between 600 and 800 years old.

The nineteenth-century Celtic Revival brought the Celtic cross back to the churchyard, and they can be seen in their hundreds in churchyards and cemeteries. The memorial at Coniston (Cumb), to John Ruskin, author and art critic, who died in 1900, is one of our most striking modern memorials. The beautifully decorated cross was carved from a single block of green stone from the Mossrigg Quarry at Tilberthwaite.

The cross commemorating Sir Thomas Moore at Bromham (Wilts) who died in 1906, dominates the north side of the church. Below the cross are Moore's own lines:

> Harp of my country in darkness I found thee,
> The cold chain of silence has hung o'er thee long,
> When proudly, my own Island harp, I unbound thee,
> And gave all my chords to light, freedom and song.

4 Pre-Reformation memorials

The churchyard memorial as we know it today is almost entirely Post-Reformation; any early survivals, if not lost under the soil, will have been taken into the church or removed to a museum. For the remainder, the effects of time, weather, neglect and destruction have resulted in the loss of the vast majority of early memorials, a process which continues today. Early wooden grave markers have succumbed to natural decay, and hundreds of small early headstones will simply have sunk beneath the soil or crumbled away. Wholesale destruction by the iconoclasts would have accounted for the rest, although many stones can still be seen built into the fabric of the church. In the tiny church of Temple, on Bodmin Moor (Cnwll), various stones bearing the engraved crosses of the Knights Templars and Hospitallers can be seen in the walls. At Beverston (Gloucs) there are four incised stone coffin lids built into the outside wall of the Berkeley Chapel in St Mary's Church and many other churches have similar examples.

Early monuments

The first individual funerary monuments date from the Roman occupation and are known as *stelae* (derived from the Greek *stele*). They were rectangular, the top square, gabled or pedimented with a recessed panel, the surround plain, or carved with architectural motifs; in the central panel there may be a figure carved in a niche or a simple inscription. In many ways they were not dissimilar from some Greek Revival headstones found in Victorian cemeteries today. A number of *stelae* survive: in the Corinium Museum at Cirencester (Gloucs) are two tombstones from the first century AD found nearby in 1835. They are carved in local stone and show mounted soldiers in battle, their names and ages inscribed beneath (see p.38). Another survival in excellent condition is the monument to L Duccius Rufinus in York Museum. Several museums have *stelae*, including Colchester (Essex) and Newcastle-upon-Tyne (T & W). Such was the importance attached to commemoration that some Romans had their tombstones carved during their lifetime.

A large number of Roman coffins survive, but the best collection is in the grounds of the Yorkshire Museum. They are massive monoliths, and the problems involved in the transport and excavation of them can only be imagined. The most outstanding survival is the coped sarcophagus found in Haydon Lane, London in 1853 and now in the British Museum. The lid is decorated with acanthus leaves and the sides carved with strigillations and a central portrait. The end panels are carved with a basket of loaves and other offerings to the gods. It contained a lead coffin decorated with scallop shells and mouldings. It can be assumed that highly ornate sarcophagi with internal coffins were not intended for

Tombstone from the first century AD to the Roman soldier Dannicus (Drawing by N Griffiths)

burial, but would have been destined for a family mausoleum or vault above ground.

Anglo-Saxon and Viking memorials

In addition to the legacy of the churchyard cross, the richness of Anglo-Saxon sculpture is amply demonstrated in churches such as Breedon-on-the-Hill (Leics), Britford and Codford St Peter (Wilts). There are said to be some 2,500 remnants of Anglo-Saxon sculpture surviving; in the church porch at Bakewell (Derbys) is a whole collection of Saxon and mediaeval stones and fragments unearthed during restoration work in 1841, indicating that Bakewell had been an important Christian centre as well as a burial site.

Surviving individual memorials are generally associated with ecclesiastical or monastic centres; in the Priory Museum at Lindisfarne (Nthumb), which less than a century after the acceptance of Christianity had become a monastic centre of Christian activity and learning, are the erroneously named pillow-stones, small identification slabs measuring about 15x20cm which were laid on the face or breast of the corpse. Similar but slightly larger stones from Hartlepool (Dur) and York Minster are inscribed with a cross of similar design and of Irish origin.

Among the most evocative pre-Conquest burial sites is the ruined cliff-top chapel of St Patrick at Heysham (Lancs), one of the earliest Christian sites in north-west England and thought to have been built in the eighth century. Right on the cliff edge are six graves cut

10 Pre-Conquest burial site at Heysham, Lancs

into the rock, two straight-sided and four body-shaped. Each is rebated to take a lid, and has a socket-hole at the head, presumably intended to take a cross shaft**(10)**. A cemetery to the south of the nearby chapel was excavated in 1977 and the skeletons found were dated to the tenth and eleventh centuries. They were reburied in the neighbouring churchyard of St Peter. Inside the church is a tenth-century hogback stone in excellent condition and a number of coffin slabs built into the walls including the gravestone of a seventeenth-century priest.

Headstones

The headstone is a natural progression from the pagan monolith and the Roman *stela*. At Bibury (Gloucs) are three, all of the Scandinavian type: one is built into the outside north wall of the chancel. Casts of another two which are in the Ringerike style of the early eleventh century are in the church; the originals are in the British Museum.

A rare Anglo-Saxon survival, in such good condition that it has probably never been outside for any length of time, is the Lechmere Stone, which is in private hands at Hanley Castle (Worcs). It is 46cm high, carved on the face with the figure of Christ wearing a pleated garment in two layers and holding a book. There is cable moulding round the edge, and on the back is a cross pattée with a baluster-like stem and pointed-leaf foliage typical of the early/middle tenth century.[1] There is a similar one at Whitchurch (Hants) with an inscription in Latin capitals commemorating Frithburga.

The shrine tomb

The shrine, or house tomb, so familiar in the archaeological museums of Florence and Rome, would seem to be derived from the continent, where the tomb, either as a metal reliquary or casket, is represented symbolically as a house or casket. According to Bede[2] the memorial to St Chad, who died in AD 670, was built of wood in the shape of a gabled house. In this country the most important surviving memorial of this type is the Hedda Stone in Peterborough Cathedral; it has six saints standing within arcading, while the gabled roof is decorated with animals and interlace.

11 Anglo-Saxon Wirksworth stone, Derbys (Wirksworth Parochial Church Council)

Coped stones

If the height of the house-tomb is reduced, the memorial becomes a coped stone, of which a few survive in whole or in part, notably in Cornwall. One of the most rewarding and atmospheric places is the churchyard of Lanivet, which is at the geographical centre of Cornwall and the hub of early routes across and along the peninsular. It is well endowed with early memorials: a pillar stone of the fifth or sixth century is inscribed ANNICU, and there is also a cross-shaft with incised decoration and a tall wheelhead cross with interlaced decoration. By the south wall of the church is one of only four hogback or coped stones in Cornwall; it has a representation of tiles or shingles on the curved surfaces and a key pattern on the sides (see p.46). There are others at Phillack and St Buryan (inside) and in the porch at St Tudy.

At Wirksworth (Derbys), now on the church wall, is the famous Wirksworth slab, an Anglo-Saxon coffin lid which was found two feet below the surface when an area in front of the altar was excavated in 1820. With the carved surface facing downwards it was covering a stone-built vault containing a large human skeleton in perfect condition, thought to be the remains of St Betti. It is a coped slab richly carved with biblical scenes which include Christ Washing the Feet of the Disciples and the Presentation at the Temple. The dumpy figures are crowded together in a frenzy of activity. It seems probable that the Cross on the upper tier was originally in the centre, in which case a sizeable piece of the stone is missing **(11)**.

Hogbacks

The Viking incursions in the north of the country have left a legacy of tombstones of the type known as hogback, a short-lived type of memorial carved with ornamental patterns and serpents significant in Norse mythology and also derived from the house-tomb. They are long and low, covering the grave longitudinally and about 0.6-1.2m high with a curved upper surface and bowed sides. At each end there are carved animals, possibly bears, facing inwards with their arms out as though embracing the stone The ones in the church at Brompton (N Yorks) even have shingles to add to the impression of a house, and are richly decorated with bands of plaitwork and spirals. They are thought to be the earliest survivals. Other hogbacks, all inside, are at Lowther and Gosforth (Cumb) and Heysham (Lancs).

In the circular churchyard at Penrith (Cumb) the collection of ancient stones known as the 'Giant's Grave' consists of two crosses and four semicircular hogbacks set in pairs. They date from the second half of the tenth century. The origin of the name comes from the legend that the stones cover the remains of Owen the Great, a famous Cumbrian king who once reigned in Penrith.

Grave slabs
The horizontal grave slab, either flat or coped, and carved only on one face, may have developed from the coffin lid of the pre-Viking period. Many are carved with a cross or have one superimposed along the ridge, thus dividing the surface into panels The Hickling (Notts) coped stone has richly carved panels, similar to some of those found in the York Minster excavations. Inside the church at Ramsbury (Wilts) are two ninth-century coped stones as well as a sepulchral slab with a Latin cross raised in relief and a lion *passant* , described by Pevsner as 'a strange conceit'.[3]

A Saxon church once stood on the site of the present church at St Minver (Cnwll) and crude slate coffins, evidence of pre-Christian burials, have been found in the churchyard.

A tenth-century grave cover, now very worn and in two parts, in the churchyard at Hackthorn (Lincs) shows traces of interlace decoration, also very worn. Nearby is a small headstone with a crudely carved cross on both faces and cable moulding round the edges; presumably the headstone was associated with the grave slab. It was discovered together with several mediaeval coffins during the digging of the foundations for a new church in 1844; in one was found a pewter chalice and paten so evidently the bodies they contained were those of priests(12). At Edgeworth (Gloucs) are two flat Anglo-Saxon stones of which one is carved with a chalice, also indicating that it commemorated a priest. They stand side by side with two Georgian headstones, an interesting juxtaposition of styles (13).

Mediaeval monuments 1066-1550

Following the Norman Conquest, with its tremendous programme of church building, there was an overlap period when many of the previous ideas persisted and the influence of the great scriptoria remained strong. The Normans believed in the conflict between the forces of good and evil, so well-illustrated in the richly carved tympana and doorways of churches such as Kilpeck (Herefs) and Quenington (Gloucs) and in the fonts at Lullington (Somset) and Southrop (Gloucs). The powers of darkness are illustrated by grotesques and dragons, writhing serpents and biting beasts, while the protection of the church is demonstrated by exuberant carvings of Christ in Majesty, the Cross and the Tree of Life.

The most common surviving Anglo-Norman memorial is the grave slab, often decorated with patterns reminiscent of the Viking period, such as the one at Burnsall with a geometric design, or another at Spennithorne (N Yorks). In the church porch at Steyning, (Sussex) is a cross slab in excellent condition with a forked design and transverse bars enclosing a central panel. A fine tapered coped slab now in the museum at Trowbridge (Wilts) has a raised cross and Latin inscription which translated reads: Hail Mary full of grace, here is buried a girl called Aceline **(14)**. Trowbridge Museum also has three other Norman coffin lids.

Pre-Reformation monuments in churchyards, not surprisingly, are rare, although many survive in museums and inside churches. In the collection of stones at Bakewell (Derbys) is a thirteenth-century slab with a simple cross-fleury, a form that was derived from heraldic design and was to become more intricate in the fourteenth and fifteenth centuries. During the great revival of church building in the fourteenth-century quarries were opened up which were able to supply stone for the increasing numbers of memorials both inside and outside the church.

Headstones
Early headstones or grave markers are small and easily overlooked. In the churchyard at Broadway (Worcs) are three stone markers, only about 18 in (46cm) high, of which two are head and footstones. They are carved with a trefoil design and inscribed in memory of Ann Davis, 1516. A pre-Reformation discoid headstone at Grantham (Lincs) has unfortunately disappeared. There are two early markers in the collection at Bakewell (Derbys).

Ledgers
A number of churchyards have surviving mediaeval coffins made of hollowed out solid blocks of stone. These would have been buried so that the lid, or ledger, often decorated with an heraldic design, was on a level with the ground. In the churchyard of Howick

13 Saxon and Georgian headstones at Edgeworth, Gloucs

Hall, Longhoughton (Nthumb) is a group of thirteenth-century slabs, one incised with a pair of shears, thought to be in their original position. There is another, carved with a chalice, outside the porch at Richmond (N Yorks) and several close to the church wall at Ashton Keynes (Wilts). A heavy stone monolith at Lower Wraxall (Wilts) has acquired a later headstone and footstone.

Under the east wall of a disused church at Caenby (Lincs) is a handsome recumbent grave slab bearing a fleury cross with a stepped base. It is in good condition and if the church is to change hands it needs to be protected. A similar one unearthed recently in the churchyard at Lydney (Gloucs) has now been taken into the church.

Another important survival is the thirteenth-century grave slab in the churchyard at Bellingham (Nthumb) known as the Lang Pack Stone. It is said to be the tomb of a robber who features in Ettrick Shepherd's *Tale of the Long Pack*. Legend has it that a pedlar came to a house in the village and left a long package. One of the servants saw it move, and called for help. The ploughboy came in and shot it, upon which blood spurted out and the bundle lay still. Later that evening he blew the silver horn found in the pack, and a band of raiders rode in and were all killed, but by the next morning all the bodies had vanished. The dead robber was buried under the Lang Pack Stone and was never identified. In the same churchyard against the wall of the chancel is a stone dated 1628 with large, widely-spaced lettering to Charlton of Redesmouth.

Under the east window of the church at Sheen (Staffs) is a full-length sepulchral slab with a decorated cross, possibly that of an early priest, Thomas de Shene. There is also a stone effigy of a priest, *c.*1450, which was probably originally inside. An unusual departure

14 *Twelfth-century coped gravestone, Trowbridge. (Wiltshire County Council Libraries and Heritage)*

in design is the fourteenth-century version of the house-tomb at Bredon (Worcs) which looks like a model church with transepts. This design was to reappear in the late nineteenth century **(15)**. On either side of the church porch at Leckhampton (Gloucs) is a group of grave covers unearthed during rebuilding work. On one side are four worn recumbent effigies, one holding a heart, two with their feet resting on dogs. The other group consists of eight coffin slabs, some with crosses at the head, estimated to date from the fourteenth century.

In the churchyard of St Buryan (Cnwll) a thirteenth-century grave slab has an unusual inscription in Norman French. In translation it reads:

> Clarice the wife of Geoffrey de Bolleit lies here. God on her soul have mercy: those who pray for her soul shall have ten days pardon.

Chest tombs

The pre-Reformation chest tomb has its origins in the house tomb and is the outside equivalent of the altar tomb inside the church, although usually without the effigy so often seen on internal monuments.

The most handsome early chest tomb and a unique and remarkable survival is the early fourteenth-century tomb at Loversall (S Yorks). It is richly carved with Decorated window tracery of various designs, as though copied from the church or from a mason's pattern book; the coped slab bears a raised sword along the ridge. Of similar design but less intricate is the fifteenth-century tomb at Bishops Cannings (Wilts) which has arcading with trefoiled heads.

Burgess mentions some 40 surviving pre-Reformation chest tombs, although it is difficult to know how many are still in existence in anything approaching a reasonable condition.[4] Those at Buckland and Fairford (Gloucs), Fulbrook and Sutton Courtenay (Oxon) and Kingston Seymour (Somset) all have quatrefoils, a reminder that the designs on churchyard tombs have their origins inside the church; the ones at Rodney Stoke (Somset) and Thrapston (Hants) have shields at the centre of the quatrefoils. At Cricklade

15 Fourteenth-century house-tomb, Bredon, Worcs

(Wilts) a quatrefoiled tomb with a heavy capstone has a later inscription and a water stoup, as though to provide water or food for the journey.

The fifteenth-century tomb at Great Moulton (Norfk) has complex alternating panels with trefoils and quatrefoils and must have been beautiful in its heyday. It was recorded in the eighteenth century: 'at the south-west corner of the churchyard is a very antique altar tomb, but no arms or inscription'.[5] Unfortunately it is now in such a state of disrepair that it is held together by an iron band. We are better informed about the chest tomb at Foulsham (Norfk), which is richly decorated with quatrefoils, mouchette wheels, diamonds and crowns. It is inscribed to 'Robart Colles Cecili his Vif', and we know from Blomefield that Colles was alive in 1505.[6]

A chest tomb at Powerstock (Dorset) is in fact a dole table, from which traditionally alms were 'doled out' to the poor. There are early dole tables at Edington and Potterne (Wilts), Dundry (N Somset), Dacre (Cumb) and one at Saintbury (Gloucs) which is now inside the church. There is no evidence as to whether dole tables were originally tombs, although it seems probable.

In the superb setting of the church at Buckden (Cambs), with the dark brick of the Bishop of Lincoln's Palace behind, is a large Gothic chest tomb with quatrefoils and shields which is said to be that of the young Duke of Suffolk, who fled the plague in 1551 but died of it in Buckden.

Under the east window of the church of St Peter and St Paul at Mulcheney (Somset), is a tall chest tomb said to have contained the headless effigy of Thomas Yve, the last prior of the ruined abbey nearby, who died in 1538. It has elegant arcading with trefoils in ogee arched panels. It was moved to its present position after it was found during excavations in 1873 and is now in poor condition.

Where effigies are found on early churchyard memorials it is usually because the monument has been moved out of the church, perhaps through lack of space, or to make room for later and more desirable incumbents. The 'double bed' memorial to the Cutts family at South Cerney (Gloucs) has effigies of a civilian and his wife side by side and is dated at 1370. Because of its condition it seems likely that it was inside the church for

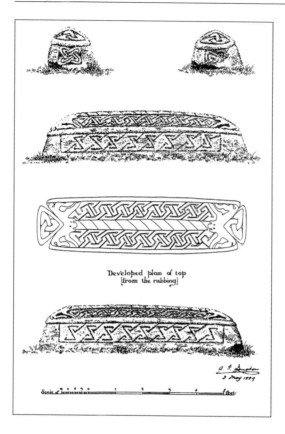

Developed plan of top
[from the rubbing]

*Coped stone in the churchyard at Lanivet Cornwall
(Langdon, Old Cornish Crosses)*

many years. There is another badly defaced late thirteenth-century pair at Berrow (Somset). The woman wearing a veil on a fourteenth-century chest tomb at Necton (Norfk) has a tasselled cushion under her head and is wearing a long dress.

The extraordinary thirteenth-century canopied tomb at Astbury (Ches) is known to have been inside the church. It has two worn recumbent figures of a man and a woman (she has lost her head) with their hands joined in prayer. They are thought to be members of the Venables family. The arch over their heads has diagonal buttresses and seventeenth century crocketed pinnacles. Nearby is a similar figure in armour on a quatrefoiled base and another on a grave slab, possibly in clerical garb. Occasionally effigies were placed in gabled recesses in the outer church wall, as at Great Brington (Hants) and Langley Burrell (Wilts).

High in the Cotswolds in the churchyard at Compton Abdale (Gloucs) is a chest tomb with a worn effigy and an incised Celtic cross and also the indentations for a game of Nine Men's Morris; a rare combination on a churchyard memorial. Nine Men's Morris, or larger merrills (merelles) was an expanded version of merrills, a board game like noughts and crosses in which the aim was to get three pieces in a row. Boards have been found on the cloister benches in Westminster Abbey and Canterbury Cathedral.[7] There is a chest tomb at Hazleton in the next parish which has a cross and an incised game, possibly of Fox and Geese, a more complex game in which the fox tries to capture the geese by jumping over them, and the geese in turn try to corner the fox. Merrills have also been found at Langford (Oxon), with deep runnels joining the holes.

Amongst the oddest mediaeval survivals are the four stone bears that are still in their original positions marking the corners of the churchyard at Dacre (Cumb). Each stands upright at about 1.2m high and each is different, telling a four-part story in mediaeval fashion. Little is known of their origin, but they are said to represent 'a humorous rendering of a bear legend'.[8]

5 Post-Reformation memorials

In the 100 years following the Reformation, churchyard memorials in stone slowly began to reappear as space for burials inside the church ran out; also more families could afford to buy burial plots in the churchyard and wanted their final resting place commemorated in some way. The development of the ornamentation and inscriptions on these memorials is worthy of study, providing details of local families, their occupations and of how and when they died, often accompanied by an epitaph. They come in all shapes and sizes, from the strictly functional, bearing a simple record of the deceased, to the ostentatious or even eccentric. From the simple headstone or plain horizontal ledger to the highly-decorated and intricately-carved chest tomb commemorating some wealthy and important personage. The greatest concentration of chest tombs is in the Cotswolds and the Severn Vale, where the combination of 'wool' wealth and oolitic limestone produced some of the grandest houses as well as the best in churchyard architecture.

Encouraged by the spread of pattern books, individual stonemasons began to develop their own styles and designs, so that in some churchyards such as Bibury (Gloucs) carved cherubs on a row of headstones seem to have a family resemblance as though they were brothers. In areas of the Midlands where signatures on slate headstones have survived the ravages of time, names such as Sparrow and Staveley can be traced through the generations as they follow the changing fashions in design. Unfortunately many slate headstones have sunk over the years, and the signature, which is usually at the bottom, has disappeared from view.

However the dating of memorials can be a precarious business. If there have been several burials the earlier dates may have eroded; often later burials, especially those of children, are inscribed on the end panels and are still legible when the inscriptions on the side panels have worn away. On the early chest tomb to Simon Holditch, dated 1602, and his wife at Thrapston (Hants) the inscription in Roman lettering is on the end panel but the sides are plain. The scene is complicated by those inscriptions which include a list of ancestors, so that the earliest date does not refer to a burial under that tomb. It is not uncommon to find headstones that have been re-used and perhaps have earlier names and dates on the back without any indication as to whether there may be a connection between the different names.

Early in the seventeenth century Weever wrote:

> Sepulchres should be made according to the quality and degree of the person deceased. Persons of plebeian sort shall be buried without any tomb or gravestone or epitaph: persons of the meanest sort of gentry a flat gravestone;

Gentlemen of more emenencie, effigies and representations cut upon a terme or pedestal, but no arms. Noblemen and princes and kings had their sepulchres raised aloft and their personages delineated, carved, embost, the full length and bigness in alabaster, rich marble... epitaphs were only for such as were of vertue, wisdom, valour.[1]

Headstones

Early headstones or grave markers are short and thick in relation to their height, with the inscription carved, often erratically, on a recessed panel on the face. A few early discoids have survived, the best being the pair at Lower Swell (Gloucs), one of which is inscribed Ann Davis, 1628.

It seems likely that in rural areas the stonemasons were not the skilled artisans of later generations, but were builders of houses, barns and stone walls, the equivalent of the general builder of today. The only person likely to have had the necessary literacy and lettering skills for carving inscriptions on gravestones would often have been the local schoolmaster. Burgess tells of a Cornish schoolmaster, William Westaway, who kept tombstones in the classroom and worked on them while teaching.[2]

Hundreds of these small stones will have disappeared beneath the soil; of those that survive most date from the seventeenth or early eighteenth century and from their simplicity we can assume that they record some of the humbler members of the community. There are good examples in the churchyards of the Forest of Dean (Gloucs), in particular at Awre, Lydney and Newland, and at Hazleton in the Cotswolds there is a row of dumpy headstones with sunken inscription plaques. In Wiltshire there are early examples at Broad Hinton, Cricklade (St Sampsons) and Etchilhampton, and a particularly attractive one dated 1697 at Melksham with an incised angel and decorative lettering. A number of early slate headstones can be found in Cornwall, often roughly incised with a skull and crossbones; in the Midlands individual slates survive at Swithland (Leics) and Grantham (Lincs).

Even in the early days of churchyard commemoration regional variations are apparent. In the northern churchyards of Yorkshire and Northumberland headstones are thicker and heavier, sometimes with crude carving on the face and the inscription on the back; at Whittingham (Nthumb) a number of headstones have widely differing dates, as though they have been re-used. There is a single small headstone in the old churchyard of Upleatham (N Yorks), and at Escomb (Dur) a small headstone has a human-looking face and stylised *memento mori*. The peaceful churchyard at Bewcastle (Cumb) has an interesting collection of headstones of all shapes and designs, some carved on both sides, some re-used, with a variety of lettering styles. An early stone has a diminutive figure of Father Time (**16**) and an enigmatic inscription:

MEMENTO MORI PUT YE IN THE SICKLE FOR THE HARVEST

16 *Father Time on a*
   headstone at Bewcastle,
   Cumbria

An interesting variation in the shape of the headstone can be seen in the churchyards of West Kent and East Sussex, where the hood of the stone was given shoulders surmounted by a small hoodmould, often with one or more deep-eyed skulls on the face. There is sometimes an S-shaped bulge on the side of the stone, adding to the anthropomorphic impression. To stand in a churchyard such as Hadlow or East Peckham (Kent) in a poor light is an eerie experience **(Plate 5)**. Interestingly, some of the inscriptions emphasise the upright stance of the stone. This example is at Boughton Monchelsea (Kent) 1688:

B

HOULD

I STAND HERE

TO TESTIFY THAT

HERE LYETH THE

BODY OF THOMAS WALK[R]

At the other end of the country the slate headstones of Cornwall have a rustic simplicity that has a particular appeal. They range from a simple skull and crossbones like a child's drawing to the sophisticated pattern book designs of Egloshayle and St Endellion.

By the early eighteenth century headstones were becoming larger and thinner, with the head or *hood* of the stone carved into decorative shapes, often incorporating an angel-head and wings. In the Cotswolds these 'angel-tops' can be seen in most rural churchyards such as Brimpsfield and Cowley (Gloucs), although there is an exception at Compton Abdale where a small horseshoe-shaped stone commemorates John Wilson, 1735. At Swinbrook (Oxon) the angels have stone scrolls close to their heads, as though they were wearing ear-

*17 Double panelled
headstone at
Tetbury, Gloucs*

muffs. The face of the stone would have a plain central panel or a more formal cartouche for the inscription, bordered with drapes or floral decoration. At Elmore (Gloucs), one of the best collections in the country and listed Grade II, is a group of forty seventeenth- and eighteenth-century headstones in a wide variety of designs, many of them in excellent condition.

Originally designed to carry a single inscription, it became practicable, perhaps for reasons of economy, for subsequent burials in the family to be recorded on the same stone, requiring more space. Stones with a double silhouette began to appear; there is a particularly attractive one at Cricklade (Wilts) and another at Tetbury (Gloucs) to the Osborne family who lost three small children close together. Interestingly, they gave the name of a dead child to a subsequent one, a practice that was common at a time of high infant mortality but is no longer fashionable (**17**). A slate headstone at Melton Mowbray, (Leics) 1749, has four circular plaques, of which only one has been filled.

Many graves would also have had footstones, small stones placed at the foot of the grave and carved simply with the initials of the deceased. In later years these were often moved close to the headstone, which defeats the purpose of marking the extent of the burial, but interments with a number of footstones still in situ can be seen at Tidcombe and Bishopstone, nr Salisbury (Wilts). A rare footstone at Beverston (Gloucs) is inscribed with the initials SH and carved with a skull and crossbones.

In the mason's yard at Great Bedwyn (Wilts) is a collection of restored eighteenth-century headstones which have been painted as a reminder of how they might have looked in their heyday (**18**). In the same village the churchyard, which has some well-carved recent memorials, has a number of headstones where traces of black paint are still visible.

The second half of the eighteenth century produced the height of excellence in

18 Restored headstone in a mason's yard at Great Bedwyn, Wilts

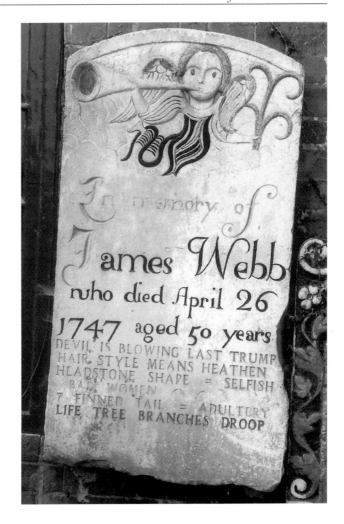

churchyard memorial architecture that we associate with the Georgian period: lavish rococo work round a central panel or cartouche, richly carved with flowers and foliage and elegant inscriptions. With the spread of pattern books and the influence of classical design the masons were able to give a free rein to their creative abilities. The hood of the stone again became plain while the sculptor turned his attention to the face of the stone.

The exuberant carving of the Georgian era is best demonstrated in the limestone belt and particularly the Cotswolds, where the most famous is the churchyard at Painswick, described by Alec Clifton-Taylor[3] as 'far more memorable indeed than the church itself'. Others at Aldsworth, Windrush and many more are richly endowed with the exuberance of rococo and baroque. At Fairford (Gloucs) is a row of elegant broad headstones carved with cherub heads, one of which, unusually, has four. In the rewarding churchyard at Linton (Herefs) rustic folk art can be seen side by side with rococo headstones in an attractive and well-maintained setting **(19)**.

Elsewhere richly-decorated eighteenth-century headstones can be found in any number of churchyards; among the best are Bridestowe and Stowford (Devon),

19 Georgian headstone at Linton, Herefs

Egloshayle (Cnwll), Long Sutton (Lincs) and Wisbech St Mary (Cambs) and and the redundant churchyard of Parson Drove in the same county, which has a fine collection of carved headstones. Two are decorated with winged angel heads in the hood and full-length weepers supporting the columns of the inscription panel **(20)**. In the slate areas of the Midlands the headstones in Swithland slate by Christopher Staveley at Melton Mowbray (Leics) and Grantham (Lincs) are outstanding, in an area where work of this period can be found in numerous churchyards.

Architectural designs with a classical pediment and angel-head supported by pilasters or columns were being produced by the slate carvers of Leicestershire and the surrounding counties. They are reminiscent of contemporary door styles, but also may have been derived from seventeenth century wooden panelling or furniture. The central panel may contain a rococo cartouche or a plain inscription panel. In some areas the stone would have a panel of decoration on the upper quarter and then be divided vertically by scrolls or husk drops to take two inscriptions. Sometimes the division of the stone was by a number of individual plaques or tondi on the surface of the stone, like the attractive headstone to the Flower family, 1815, at Chilmark (Wilts).

The early nineteenth century brought a uniformity of stone in shape and size. The outline was plain on a larger, thinner stone, with the decoration confined mostly to the head of the stone. All the classical symbols of mortality which were fashionable at the time, such as the draped urn, would be carved in low relief, with the word in the head of the stone such as 'Sacred' or 'In Memory' highly decorated in calligraphic style. Gradually the

20 Headstones at Parsons Drove, Cambs. (photo Christopher Dalton)

severity of the Greek Revival began to supercede the rococo as designs followed those appearing on interior church monuments: swags and garlands, urns, sarcophagi and pyramidions all carved in low relief. Cherub heads gave way to full-length angels in diaphanous drapes, grieving widows leant on coffins, and inscriptions became increasingly sentimental.

The largest single collection of eighteenth- and nineteenth-century headstones is at the redundant church of St George Reforne, Portland (Dorset) where the working quarry forms a backdrop to the churchyard. Here there are headstones of every possible design from the mid-eighteenth to the early twentieth century, rich in sculpture and local history, family tragedies and seafaring disasters such as Richard Otter who was lost on the Titanic.

By the second half of the nineteenth century the effects of improved transport and communications meant the beginning of the end of much of the individual work of carvers as churchyard memorials became standardised. The lancet-shaped stone, the ubiquitous cross and that symbol of the Victorian obsession with privacy, the kerbed grave and the railed plot, appeared in serried ranks in the expanding cemeteries. The High Street monumental masons supplied marble in a variety of colours with machine-made lettering; open books and inscribed hearts recorded the deceased, marble angels raised benedictory arms over the dead. The day of the humble, hand-carved headstone was over.

Ledgers
Historically, horizontal slabs or ledgers are almost as old as headstones. Every church has ledgers covering interments underneath the floor, but in churchyards the vast majority will have sunk beneath the soil. They may have originated from the fear that the souls of

the dead would return to haunt the living. Certainly in later years the object was to prevent the activities of the 'resurrection men' or bodysnatchers. Recently in the churchyard at Tewkesbury Abbey (Gloucs) a ledger was unearthed a good 15cm beneath the grass. It recorded the death of Giles Smith in 1724; the inscription reads:

> Ingenious Giles is here lay'd down to sleep
> In hopes with Christ in heav'n to meet.

Many churchyards have raised ledgers, where the slab has been raised a foot or two on stone blocks, presumably to keep it clear of the encroaching vegetation. Except in the Cotswolds, where many of them have decorative and delicately inscribed brass plates, they generally have no decoration and no aesthetic value and are not to be confused with chest tombs, which are hollow and have completely different proportions. However in the churchyard at Grantham (Lincs) are a few memorials which seem to be a local variation of the raised ledger; they have a coped capping stone with the gable end decorated with reeding and a central urn in high relief. The end of the lower stone has miniature acanthus scrolls flanking the inscription, which is eroded. The design would appear to be late eighteenth century.

By contrast, the slate ledgers of the West Country and Yorkshire are an art form all of their own, and many, like those at Rock and Poundstock (Cnwll) are now inside the churches for safe keeping. One of the most attractive is the slate ledger at St Enodoc (Cnwll) which used to cover a brick tomb in the churchyard and is now in the porch. It has engaging portraits of John Mably and his daughter in period costume and is said to be the latest known incised slab with effigies; the date is 1687. There are others at Saltash, Padstow (Cnwll) and also at Lew Trenchard and Stowford (Devon).

There is an outstanding collection of seventeenth- and eighteenth-century slate raised ledgers in the churchyard of St Mary's, Morley (W Yorks) and another large collection set in the ground at Lightcliffe in the same area **(Plate 6)**.

In the churchyard at Leyland (Lancs) is an early raised ledger over the grave of William Walker. On the slab is an inscribed primitive life-size figure which has the charm and simplicity of a child's drawing. Round the margin of the stone on all four sides is written:

> HEARE LIETH THE BODIE OF
> WILLIAM WALKER BATCHELOR OF
> MVSICKE CLARKE OF THIS
> PARISHE OF LEYLAND FOR
> THE SPACE OF XXV YEARES AND
> DYED THE XX OF APRIL 1588

It is a pity that the tomb has been repaired with cement, instead of limestone mortar.

A variation of the ledger is the coped stone or bodystone, which mimics the shape of the grave mound. They are tapered at both ends and rounded in cross-section. Early ones are usually without head or footstones, like the group at Wylyle or the ones at Mere (both

Wilts) which are decorated with heraldic emblems. There are a number in Kent churchyards; an odd pair at West Peckham are raised on coffin-shaped slabs and seem to be associated with a single headstone. In the churchyard at Great Bradley (Suffk) is a group of coped stones carved with gruesome cadavers. They have head and foot stones and are dated 1698. In the same group is a most attractive rococo headstone with a skull in the head carved with the initials W D, 1681.

In some areas, notably the south-east, where good freestone was not readily available, a type of memorial known as a graveboard appeared. A board, supported at each end by upright posts, covered the length of the grave. The posts were often carved into finials; some had iron spikes along the top edge. Being made on the whole of wood, graveboards have generally disintegrated with age, although a few can still be found in the churchyards of Surrey and Sussex. There is a pair, bleached silver with age, in the emotive churchyard at Stoke Poges (Bucks). At Horsted Keynes (Sussex) is a seventeenth-century stone graveboard with handsome polyhedral finials. Later ones survive at Baldock (Herts) to a boy killed in an accident, Cowden (Kent) to Flora Turner, 1884, Mickleham (Surrey) 1867 and at Wargrave (Berks) 1862. There are modern ones at Stanton St Quintin (Wilts) and Thursley (Surrey).

A variation of the graveboard, looking more like a bedstead, where the board stands across the head of the grave, can be found in Devon, at Broadwoodwidger and Lew Trenchard. They are evidently a local version of the graveboard.

Chest tombs

The chest tomb is the outside equivalent of the altar tomb inside the church, which in its turn was derived from the wooden shrines built as reliquaries for saints. The altar tomb was designed as a base for an effigy, but effigies on churchyard memorials are rare; those that exist are likely to have been moved from within the church as other, more recent and perhaps wealthier interments laid claim to the interior.

In addition to those already mentioned (see pp.45, 46) there are effigies outside at Bromsgrove (Worcs), Otley (W Yorks), and Hartpury (Gloucs), where the Sloper memorial, 1703, on its attractive oval chest tomb, is very worn. In much better condition is the memorial at Oddington (Gloucs) where the effigy of Margaret Parsons, 1695, has been reclining with her feet sticking out into the sun for over three hundred years. In the churchyard at Stone (Staffs) is the tomb of William Crompton, who died in 1603 and his wife, he in armour, she in period dress, on a plinth decorated with coats of arms and surrounded by spear-head railings. The memorial is on its original site in the chancel of the former Priory Church, which was demolished in 1758. Unfortunately William has lost both legs below the knee, supposedly at the time of the demolition. The most striking effigy is that at Stonham Aspall (Suffk), where the life-size figure of an eighteenth-century gentleman reclines on one elbow, legs crossed, as though quaffing a glass of mead. He is dressed in all the finery of the period, including a curled wig, and resting on a bulging sarcophagus with large volutes.

Of a later date is the elegant memorial to Grace Darling in the churchyard at Bamburgh

(Nthumb). She was the daughter of the Longstone lighthouse-keeper and became famous when in September 1838 she went out in a rowing boat to rescue survivors from the wreck of the *Forfarshire*. She died of consumption in 1842, aged 27.

Chest tombs are often called table tombs, although strictly speaking table tombs have a ledger at ground level and a second raised on side panels or legs. They are derived from the arcosolium or recessed arch of Roman architecture, frequently seen inside churches. There is a tall granite table tomb at Lydford (Devon) which because of its heavy construction is reminiscent of the henge of prehistory. At Lew Trenchard (Devon) is a massive granite table tomb on granite piers. The sides of the ledger are carved with scrolls and skulls in relief; on the top are two large coats of arms in high relief, now very worn, and a depression which may once have held a slate inscription panel. The church leaflet states that, in the words of antiquarian Sabine-Gould, Squire and Rector of Lew Trenchard for 43 years in the nineteenth century:

> John Wood, died 1623, arms Wood with Trelawney, as his second wife of Sibella, a daughter of John Trelawney of Trelance. There was also his plate here but it has been gone thence 100 years and more.[4]

At Gunwalloe (Cnwll) where the sea laps against the churchyard wall, is a true table tomb on four legs. A more elegant one at Malmesbury (Wilts) has ogee arches on the side panels; there is a plain one at Cranham (Gloucs), where shears carved on the tower indicate that the church was built with 'wool' money. A local variation can be seen at Corsham and Wroughton (Wilts), where a table tomb in each churchyard has reeded columns supporting the ledger; in the central space is an urn which at Corsham is carved with military trophies and at Wroughton is surrounded by stone drapes supporting an inscription plaque **(21)**. They are more common in the north, where they are usually lower on the ground with short bulbous legs, like the one at Ripley (N Yorks) which has six legs. An occasional variation of the table tomb occurs in the north, where a few tombs have concave sides so that the side panels almost meet in the middle. There are examples at Masham and Upleatham (N Yorks). Also at Upleatham is a tomb with convex end panels and a single central slab joining the two. There is a similar one at Yarm (N Yorks).

Chest tombs, on the other hand, are hollow boxes, usually in the shape of a double cube and resting on a plinth. They developed because of the need to raise the ledger above the encroaching vegetation, but also because the larger bulk of the tomb gave it greater importance among the surrounding headstones and so provided additional surfaces for decoration.

Early chest tombs were heavy in construction, the uprights supporting the ledger often a foot or more in thickness. The side panels were attached with iron bands, although in recent years stainless steel is used for repairs. Generally they have a narrow body with a heavy ledger above, the underside cut away to meet the body of the tomb. This construction can be seen on the Thorne tomb at Cucklington (Somset), 1617, where the side panels are missing. The adjacent tomb appears to be of similar date but is more than half sunk; it needs rescuing.

21 *Table tomb,*
    Wroughton,
    Wilts

A few chest tombs survive from the sixteenth and early seventeenth century; they are usually restricted in design with strongly cut lettering. There is one at Alderley (Gloucs) dated 1589 with a deeply cut inscription to John Stanton, Minister 'who after his exile for religion began to preach the gospel of Christ in this parish.' A beautiful tomb in remarkable condition at Podimore (Somset) commemorates John Swadel the Elder who died in 1593 and his son, also John who died in 1617 **(22)**. On a tomb at Miserden (Gloucs) the inscription is still legible after nearly four-hundred years:

HEARE WEARE BURIED THE BODYS OF
ANTHONY HOCKHOVLD AND TACEY HIS WIFE
WHICH ANTHONY DECEASED THE 24 OF MAY 1605
AND TACEY THE 15 OF JANVARY 1612.

There are other early chest tombs at Closworth, 1609, and South Brewham (S Somset) 1618, where the tomb is sunk and the north panels are falling in. More sophisticated is the very early tomb at Castle Cary to John Cosenes who died in 1590. It has an inscribed frieze below the ledger and under it a course of dentilled moulding.

During the seventeenth century designs became more ambitious, with fielded and arched panels, reeded pilasters and friezes. In the clifftop churchyard of Morwenstow (Cnwll) is the granite tomb in Renaissance style to John Manning, who died in 1601. Legend has it that he was killed by a bull and his wife was so shocked by the tragedy that she died in childbirth. A highly-decorated tomb at Northleach (Gloucs) is rectangular in plan with rounded ends, a very unusual design for the period. The inscription plaques have richly-scrolled surrounds and it is carved all over with cherubs and skulls, drapes and open books.

22 Early chest tomb at Podimore, Somerset, 1593

Burgess[5] describes a group of tombs at Darley Dale (Derbys) from the early seventeenth century which seem to have disappeared. Two were decorated with tracery in the Gothic style; the third, commemorating a weaver, was carved on all sides with the tools of the trade, including a loom and spinning wheel. A similar fate has befallen the tomb at Closworth (Somset) to Thomas Purdue, a bell-founder whose tomb was carved with a bell and who died in 1711. If all these memorials have disappeared, it is a sad and irreplaceable loss.

A group of neighbouring churchyards in the Forest of Dean (Gloucs) provide good examples of the development of design over a relatively short period, all in Forest stone. Three chest tombs at Lydney all have heavy capping stones and two have inscriptions in naive lettering. The third has end panels carved in high relief with rosettes and drapes. The group at Woolaston have enriched sunken panels with moulded pilasters and Roman lettering, in contrast to a later tomb at St Briavels which is deeply carved in relief with guilloche decoration and has elliptical panels with moulded surrounds. The ends are decorated with drapes and an intricate armorial bearing. Unfortunately the tomb is partially sunk and is falling in on the south side.

Very different is an adjacent memorial dated 1668 which is plain to the point of austerity apart from inscribed spearheads and coils on the east end. The inscription commemorates Matthew Butler who was messenger to two kings, Charles I and Charles II. From the same period but later in design is the tomb at Hewelsfield, which has heavy gadrooned quarter balusters and a cartouche with a cherub head.

Sometimes a find can be so unexpected and so out of place as to be startling. The church of St Peter at Plemstall (Ches) is at the end of a long lane, past an ancient well named after St Plegmund, a hermit monk who became Archbishop of Canterbury in 890 and died in 914. The churchyard is full of trees and birdsong, with modest headstones

23 Gadrooned chest tomb at Plemstall, Cheshire, 1670

leaning gently; a bulbous sundial commemorates two men who were churchwardens in 1730. At the east end of the church is a large paved area covering the vault of the Hurleston family, and on it stands an elaborate Baroque tomb on an scrolled plinth. It is the monument to Elizabeth Hurleston who died in 1670. The side panels have reclining skeletons in a rectangular frame flanked by acanthus scrolls; crossed palm fronds are carved on the end panels and the ledger has a gadrooned border **(23)**. Standing against the wall of the church is an elaborate Baroque monument with reeded pilasters and acanthus scrolls over a gadrooned base. On the pediment is a heraldic shield flanked by urns.

Towards the end of the seventeenth century and into the next, memorials are found in family groups, often close together and of similar design. Long Ashton (Somset) has a long row to the Whiting family, all the same size and of similar Renaissance design. At Castle Combe (Wilts), where there is a shuttle and scissors carved on the tower, is a large group of eighteenth-century memorials with finely carved foliate panels and quarter balusters. In the beautiful setting of the churchyard at Brympton d'Evercy (Somset) is a group of sixteenth-, seventeenth- and eighteenth-century monuments in Ham stone. Most of the chest tombs have semi-circular arched panels with imposts, keystones and dentil moulding, a plain frieze and coped ledger. A headstone in the same group has an inscription in Latin dated 1673. In a separate section of the churchyard is a large number of nineteenth-century curbed memorials, each with a plain cross and each grave completely filled with a neatly trimmed box hedge. One smaller one marks a child's grave. It is difficult to imagine what disaster overtook the household of Brympton d'Evercy.

The large group of 12 Phillimore tombs at Upper Cam (Gloucs) are impressive in their sheer solidity. Set close together and individually unexciting they reflect the importance of a local dynasty of clothiers over 150 years. In contrast there is a group of chest tombs and headstones to the Moore family at Kilmersdon (Somset). They are most attractively

24 Chest tomb with sarcophagus, Bremhill, Wilts 1837

carved with ornamental panels and friezes with rosettes, and one has slate inserts prettily inscribed. They are dated from 1622 to 1720; unfortunately they are completely ruined by the siting of the oil tank and its associated pipework.

The period from the middle of the eighteenth to the early nineteenth century is characterised by the predominance of the classical style, led by the brothers Robert and James Adam, whose first pattern book was published in 1773. Churchyard memorials took on a greater elegance, the sides of chest tombs often bellied, cartouches surrounded by rococo carving. Weeping figures and urns predominated, usually in low relief as classical imagery became more adventurous. There are several good groups including those at Corsham and Steeple Ashton (Wilts), Netherbury (Dorset) and Stinchcombe (Gloucs). On a chest tomb at Bremhill (Wilts) to the Vines family, 1837, the end is carved with coiled volutes and a sarcophagus in low relief, looking not unlike a modern wheelie-bin **(24)**.

A beautiful chest tomb at Dymock (Gloucs), is said to be a dole tomb (see p. 45) where until late in the nineteenth century the agricultural wages were paid out on Sundays. The excellent church leaflet comments that it was one way of getting the congregation to church. It is a beautiful rococo tomb to William Smith, who died in 1746, a good example of mid-eighteenth-century design.

The most sophisticated reminder of the classical influence is the monument to David Ricardo MP at Hardenhuish on the outskirts of Chippenham (Wilts). It was built in 1823, just before the influx of revival styles which swamped the classical tradition. It consists of four almost naked young men round a Corinthian column; above is a Grecian canopy with acroteria on four Doric columns and topped by an urn. The monument is surrounded by its original railings; it is the only exterior monument of this style and quality in the country, and as such is one of our most important churchyard memorials **(Plate 7)**.

Throughout this period plain, unadorned memorials continued to be made for those whose inclination or pocket ran to simpler, more dignified tastes. Perhaps they were the preferred choice of the customer, or the decision was governed by the restrictions of expense or the limitations of the material used. Every churchyard will have examples with fielded panels, quarter balusters and unassuming inscriptions. Their austerity of design and sheer solidity seems to reflect the temperament of the ordinary, hardworking and sincere members of the community.

The Cotswold chest tomb

In an area extending from the Oxfordshire Cotswolds to the Severn Vale is a concentration of remarkable work from the late seventeenth century to the mid-eighteenth. If the area is divided by a line running from Cirencester to Winchcombe the memorials can be divided neatly into the 'bale' tombs of the eastern half and the 'flamboyant' tombs of the west. In addition a third category found in all areas is the early plain tomb, sometimes modestly decorated with a simple arcade of arched panels, or with lozenges or dentils. Often a large area is given over to the inscription. There are several at Upton St Leonard's, where a particularly rich collection of memorials demonstrates the development of design over three hundred years from seventeenth century memorials with complex mouldings above raised lozenges or panels, to the variations of the lyre end of the flamboyant tomb. There is a large group at Haresfield with inscriptions in bold lettering carved between horizontal lines.

Bale tombs
Bale tombs are so called because the ledger is covered by a semi-cylindrical capping stone which was thought at one time to represent a corded bale of wool. However, many bale tombs are not those of wool merchants, and a later alternative explanation is that the shape represents the pall draped over the hearse during the funeral service. This theory is borne out by tombs at Asthall and Burford which have finials at each end of the bale corresponding to candle-holders on the hearse. The baroque tomb at Burford commemorates Robert Aston, Innholder, who died in 1698; it has three pilasters carved with fruit in high relief and a central putto. It originally had three vase finials, but the central one is lost.

The earlier tombs have a bale that is smaller than the ledger it sits on. The grooves on the bale usually run diagonally; on some tombs the bale is split in the middle and the

25 A pair of bale tombs, 1675, at Bibury, Gloucs

opposing grooves run indifferent directions; on a few they are transverse. The concave ends of the bale are usually filled with a cherub-head, an hourglass or a scallop; on two neighbouring tombs at Bibury is a pair of heavy-jowled female heads looking like disgruntled sisters **(25)**. In the same churchyard is a group of tombs showing interesting variations on the design of the bale stone. One of them commemorates Robert Day, Clerk, who died in 1784.

The earliest and most important group of bale tombs is at Broadwell and dates from the late sixteenth century and early seventeenth century. The Shayler tomb has an arcade of four arches beneath dentil moulding, each with a kneeling mourner (known colloquially as a 'weeper') with hands clasped in prayer. The bale stone has scalloped ends. This is an exceptionally sophisticated tomb for the early seventeenth century and is listed Grade I as an indication of its importance. The six Chadwell monuments have round-arched panels with keystones divided by columns and decorated with the Chadwell arms. Nearby is a pair of sixteenth-century tombs, also to the Chadwell family, one dated 1577.

A few memorials have gadrooned bales; the best is the tomb at Fairford to Valentine Strong, 1662, whose chest tomb is, unusually, solid, as opposed to the empty-box construction of the majority of chest tombs. The Strong family owned the Taynton quarries and built several of the large Cotswold houses. Valentine's sons, Thomas and

26 Three-decker bale tomb, 1727, at Shipton-under-Wychwood, Oxon

Edward worked with Wren on the rebuilding of St Paul's **(Plate 8)**. Another mason, John Kempster, 1756, has a gadrooned bale tomb at Burford. Also at Burford is a modern replica of a bale tomb, built in 1903. It has high relief carving and a frieze with a Latin inscription. In the western end of the bale is an earlier relief carving of the crucifixion, rarely seen on churchyard memorials.

The most elaborate bale tomb is the one at Windrush to Annathe Newman, who died in 1713. It has large quarter balusters carved with acanthus leaves; the bale stone has three bands of plain moulding and the ends have huge scallops — the east one with a flower, the west with a carved head and ram's horns covering the cheeks.

The Oxfordshire Cotswolds also have good collections of bale tombs, Particularly at Shilton and Swinbrook, where the early eighteenth-century headstones have 'ear-muff' angel-tops. An unusual tomb at Shipton-under-Wychwood is a rare 'triple-decker,' the only churchyard memorial of its kind. It has a large fluted bale stone and fielded panels and is richly decorated on all sides with carving in high relief in three layers. It commemorates Henry Morgan who died in 1727, and his son Robert and his wife who died in 1759 and 1734 respectively **(26)**.

Flamboyant tombs
Flamboyant tombs is the name given colloquially to the highly ornate memorials found in the western Cotswolds and the Severn Vale, an area based on the Painswick school of masons. These included John Bryan and Thomas Hamlett, both of whom are buried in Painswick churchyard under sharply contrasting memorials. John Bryan, who died in 1787, is buried under a high, severely plain pyramid based on the Caius Cestius Pyramid in Rome. By contrast Thomas Hamlett who died in1783 lies under a modest headstone which is carved with the Masons' Arms flanked by masons' tools **(27)**.

The main feature of the flamboyant tomb is the adaptation of the end panels into the

27 Headstone to Thomas Hamlett, 1783, Master Mason at Painswick, Gloucs

attractive shape known as the 'lyre end.' This was achieved by adding an S-shaped bracket or console to the sides of the rectangular end panel, so that the outline loosely resembles that of a lyre.

The console resembles the volute of the Ionic capital, a typical feature of Italian Renaissance architecture that was brought to this country by Inigo Jones in the early seventeenth century. John Summerson describes it as 'of a hitherto unfamiliar type, with curved (concave) sides and flat tops carrying pediments. Further, the moulded edges of the gables were voluted at their lower ends, giving a suggestion of classical volutes'.[6] It first appeared as an architectural feature in about 1619; it was called the Holborn gable after two houses in Holborn where the design first appeared (see p.67). It was said to have been brought from Holland by Nicholas Stone, a leading stonemason and associate of Inigo Jones, who arrived from Amsterdam in 1613. It rapidly became popular and can be seen throughout the country on door pediments, overmantels and on interior church monuments. On the Cotswold chest tomb a feature which was intended as an architectural support had become not only inverted, but purely decorative, and is an interesting example of masons converting designs from the classical houses of the period for their own purposes **(28)**.

The variation of the lyre console makes an interesting study in its own right, depending on the skill of the stonemason and the wishes and the purse of the client. From the merest suggestion of a scroll they progress with increasing vigour to the full-blown console richly decorated with acanthus leaves and cherub-heads. In between are a variety of sizes and decoration, from the most restrained, with modest volutes only projecting a matter of inches at the bottom, through to the most flamboyant, wide at the bottom and curling out

28 *Lyre-ended tombs at Haresfield, Gloucs*

at the top, often with projecting leaves or gadrooning half way up.

The end panel, flanked by the consoles, is often deeply carved with cherub-heads, heraldic emblems and clusters of foliage and fruit. On a few tombs the volute also appears on the side, usually flanking the inscription panel. It is flatter and undecorated in form, described by Elliott[7] as a 'scimitar,' and appears on a number of memorials including the chest tomb to a soldier at Kingscote (see p.122) and the beautiful tomb to William Atkyns, 1670, at Upton St Leonards where the lyre end can be seen in all its stages of development. Interestingly, the reverse of the console adjacent to the side panels of the memorial is always left undecorated **(Plate 9)**. On the north side of the church are two adjacent memorials to the Ocknold family. The earlier one, dated 1657 is an austere monument in the Jacobean style, narrow-bodied with a broad capping stone. Beneath a wide band of mouldings the sides are carved into an arcade of four arches divided by balusters pinched at the waist; the ends have a single arch. The second tomb, erected only thirty-two years later in 1689, demonstrates the change to the Baroque; it has a restrained lyre end and a fielded inscription panel flanked by scrolls very similar to those on the Atkyns memorial.

The churchyard also has examples of local styles, perhaps the work of a single stonemason, which are almost unique to that churchyard. The lyre ends are modestly executed, usually with a restrained cartouche; some volutes are decorated with flat-leaf carving, very different from the exuberance of other churchyards nearby **(29)**.

There are four churchyards which are exceptional for the quality and quantity of their memorials yet within a small area have considerable variations of style. Painswick, with its outstanding collection of Georgian tombs, is head and shoulders above the rest. This is due to a combination of factors: the affluence of its inhabitants who were able to afford what must have been expensive and time-consuming work, the availability of high-quality stone from the surrounding quarries, and the skills of local stonemasons. The work at Painswick has an air of formality about it; plump cherubs stand holding heavy tasselled drapes as though posed for a photograph; the group of Poole tombs, 1798, is a good example. The

churchyard with its trimmed yews is beautifully maintained and the fascinating and detailed Tomb Trail leaflet does much to encourage an interest in the memorials.

By contrast, Elmore, Haresfield and Standish have work of a similar standard but generally earlier and in a more relaxed style with a broader use of imagery. Trees overhang, birds sing, stone weepers recline or even doze, like the one on the Birt tomb at Haresfield. Also at Haresfield three flamboyant tombs in a row to the Niblett family are so close together that the inner side panels have been spared by the elements and are in an excellent condition of preservation. At Standish the beautiful tomb, also to the Niblett family, 1676, has weepers lounging on toothy skulls beneath rich swags of fruit; the Nibletts must have been a family of considerable wealth and importance.

Other churchyards with flamboyant tombs include Stonehouse, where the river that once drove the mills runs through the churchyard, and where there is a wide variety of memorials of all types; also Coaley, Daglingworth, Slimbridge, Tetbury, Stinchcombe and Upper Cam. At Sapperton a beautiful Grade II★ tomb is in danger of collapse. Where the Cotswolds extend into Wiltshire the Adye tomb at Easton Grey is an isolated outlier. The Adye family held the manor at Easton Grey in the early eighteenth century and the exceptional quality of the memorial reflects their status. It has gadrooned quarter balusters with coiled volutes at the base; full length cherubs support a rococo cartouche and the ends are deeply carved with the symbols of mortality at one end and two heads holding an heraldic emblem at the other. The inscription to John Adye, who died in 1731 reads:

> He gave by his last will eight shillings yearly to be disposed of in bread on Christmas Day by ye minister and churchwardens to the poor of this parish for ever.

My Ladye Cooke's House, Holborn

Also in Wiltshire at Minety is a lyre-end chest tomb, its side panels richly carved with cavorting cherubs with books and skulls flanking a plain central panel.

Weepers are an attractive feature of many Cotswold chest tombs. If they are associated with a skull, either holding it or with a foot resting on it, they are thought to represent children who have died. In the village of Cowley the Briggs memorial, 1709, has full-length figures in contemporary dress; at Bourton-on-the-Water the Jordan bale tomb, 1771, has statuettes in half relief on either side of a rectangular inscription panel. At Elmore and Hardwicke they trail scarves; at Elkstone the Poole memorial, 1692, has weepers sitting on enlarged skulls which are themselves on coiled volutes. The churchyards of Upton St Leonards, Elmore, Haresfield, Harescombe and Stonehouse and several others all have a rich variety. In the churchyard at Lea (Herefs) the Yearsley memorial has lyre ends and figures in long scarves and pantaloons with a decidedly eastern flavour.

In the Cotswolds four chest tombs have portraits: Daglingworth, Harescombe, where there is one at each end, and Leighterton. The one at Bourton-on-the-Water is in poor

30 Palling memorial, 1758, Painswick, Gloucs

condition. There are others, such as the early eighteenth-century lyre-end chest tomb at Longney which could well be portraits, but have not been identified as such.

Complete skeletons are rare, perhaps because the level of expertise required must have been time-consuming and therefore expensive, but they can be seen with total anatomical accuracy on chest tombs at Painswick, Standish and Elmore.

In the eastern half of the Cotswolds there are only a few lyre-end tombs, all of the restrained variety and hardly noticeable as such. In the overmown churchyard at Quenington, on the dividing line between east and west is a pair of chest tombs to the Thomas family dated 1677 and 1685; these are the only memorials that have both the lyre end and the bale.

Throughout the period from 1650 to 1800 when the craft of the memorial carver was at its peak, other forms of decoration were emerging which did not necessarily include the bale or the lyre end, or where the coiled volute has been reduced in significance. Gadrooned balusters were a feature of many chest tombs, with beautiful examples at Elmore and Standish, the end panels carved with symbolic emblems or cartouches, and filled with shields, flowers and fruit. The side panels were decorated with a variety of rococo cartouches, or rectangular and oval panels, often with cherub-heads in the spandrels.

By the second half of the eighteenth century extravagantly decorated memorials were being superseded by a type sometimes called 'transitional'. Designs had moved on from the traditional double cube to the Georgian elegance of a taller chest tomb, often with a moulded capping stone. There are many superb examples including those at Boxwell, Minchinhampton, North Nibley, Painswick, and Pitchcombe. In the churchyard at Tetbury is a richly decorated mid-eighteenth-century chest tomb with gadrooned baluster ends and egg-and-dart moulding. The large capping stone has scrolled ends and a rectangular finial, the sides carved with cherub heads and skulls. At Painswick the beautiful Palling memorial, 1758, which has recently been restored, has a single scroll at

31 'Tea-caddy' to John Packer, Clothier, 1733, at Painswick, Gloucs

each end, one carved with a bat-winged skull, and a delicate frieze below a flat ledger **(30)**.

Weaver, in his book *Memorials and Monuments* published in 1915, has photographs of many of the Painswick memorials in their earlier splendour, including the Palling memorial surrounded by railings, and the oldest chest tomb commemorating Gyles Smith, 1707, its sculpture still in good condition.

The churchyard memorials of the Cotswolds have a richness of variety, skill and humour that is a reflection of the affluence of the area. Attention is rightly centred on Painswick, where the combination of the churchyard, its trees and the village itself forms a uniquely picturesque setting. However there is much of interest in almost every Cotswold churchyard, and in particular those of the Severn Vale, where small parishes are struggling to preserve the treasures of church and churchyard.

Pedestal tombs
Pedestal tombs are an eighteenth-century variation of the chest tomb which, as the name suggests, are taller than they are wide, the base usually being square, rectangular or round. Square or rectangular ones have lids stepped in decreasing sizes; the round ones have a true dome, often with a finial. The round pedestals are found most often in the Cotswolds, and are affectionately known as 'tea-caddies;' **(31)** they can be seen at their best at Painswick, where they are reputed to be the work of the Bryan family. There is a

particularly elegant one at Uley with a fluted dome and supporting side consoles bearing miniature carvings of an urn and an obelisk. The central plaque is surmounted by a finely-carved drooping sheaf of foliage. It commemorates John Dimery, Clothier, who died in 1801.

Somewhere in between the chest tomb and the pedestal tomb are memorials that have a capping stone in a series of mouldings described by Burgess as 'like the lid of a casket'. They appear in every churchyard and usually date from the middle of the eighteenth century and well into the next. On the fringe of the Cotswolds at Sherston (WIlts) is a handsome memorial to Estcourt-Cresswell, 1823, with husk drops on the pilasters and a scalloped edge above a frieze. There is Italian and Roman lettering on the inscription panels, all painted in black, and the memorial is surrounded by handsome railings with corner urns **(32)**.

There are several of square and rectangular plan at Fairford, where the memorial to the Luckman family, 1792, is one of the most elegant. It has a stepped lid with roll moulding at the top; below that is a reeded frieze interspersed with rosettes. The front panel has a delicate border of scrolls and flowers with the inscription finely lettered. Another good group with an attractive uniformity of design is at Winson, commemorating the Bridges and Howse families. They are nearly all from the second half of the eighteenth century and have gadrooned corner balusters and moulded capping stones. Nearby is a modern slate by Bryant Fedden commemorating Walter Field, 'for forty years carpenter and wheelwright in this parish and devoted servant of the church and Elizabeth his wife who was postmistress for thirty-five years'. They died in 1961 and 1951 respectively.

On the southern edge of the Cotswolds at Kington St Michael (Wilts) is a handsome pedestal tomb with egg-and-dart moulding and a heraldic plaque bearing the arms of the Yealfe family. It forms part of a large group of eighteenth-century chest tombs.

By the early nineteenth century the larger style of pedestal tomb had become very popular and can be found in nearly every churchyard. There is an elegant row at Hardwicke with seated weepers and trailing sheaves of foliage, said to be the work of John Pearce of Frampton-on-Severn. He was also responsible for a characteristic 'cauliflower' tree with an unhappy weeping cherub seated underneath; seen on large pedestal tombs at Frampton and Arlingham.

Monuments

Monuments are taller and more pretentious than pedestals and generally have a chest tomb base topped by a podium or finial, or often both. The design is usually of classical origin and can be very elegant or can verge on the ostentatious. Sometimes they incorporate a sarcophagus. One of the earliest is the tomb of the poet Edmund Waller who died in 1687 at Beaconsfield (Bucks) which consists of a tall marble obelisk set on four winged skulls. It is mounted on a large chest tomb base the top half of which is covered by stone drapery of a darker colour, creating a strange effect. There are flaming urns on the four corners and the monument is surrounded by spearhead railings. In complete contrast is the huge monument to Thomas Gray, designed by Wyatt, which is outside the churchyard at Stoke Poges (Bucks) and does not contain his remains (see p.132).

At Burton Lazars (Leics) is the elaborate memorial to William Squire who died in 1781,

32 Lidded chest tomb,1823, at Sherston, Wilts

leaving half his modest fortune of £600 to be spent on the monument. The rectangular chest tomb base has a three-stepped oval plinth; at each end is a circular pier carved with the symbols of death and surmounted by a globe. The corners are decorated with volutes and husk drops. Above, a sarcophagus with an oval panel at each end and pie-crust edging stands on classical volutes. Above this again, a tall obelisk with concave sides stands on four balls. It is richly decorated: in the south face is an oval opening containing an urn while the figures of Faith and Hope recline against the sides. The monument is approximately six metres high and occupies a dominant position in the corner of the churchyard **(Plate 10)**.

In the churchyard at Tetbury (Gloucs) are two monuments of startling contrast, although of a similar period. Behind the church and in danger of being obscured by a holly tree is the elegant memorial to Sarah Paul who died in 1796. The chest tomb has crossed trumpets and crossed torches on the east and west panels respectively, and oval inscription panels with egg-and-dart moulding and fluted pilaster strips. Above is a carved frieze with reeding broken by patera. On top of the chest stands a pyramid on four feet topped by an urn **(33)**. The second large and elaborate monument stands facing the main gate to the churchyard. It has a wide stepped base and plinth, on which rests the bellied sarcophagus; it is lavishly decorated with acanthus leaves and cherub heads, with a heavily gadrooned lid. Above is a moulded plinth with Corinthian half-capitals on each side of eroded inscription panels. The eight-point gadrooned finial which would have topped the monument is on the ground and damaged **(34)**. These two monuments provide an interesting comparison between the exuberance of the Baroque and the restrained Georgian elegance of the Paul tomb.

Also in the baroque style is the monument to Captain Day who died in 1790 which

33 (left) Elegant monument to the Paul family, 1796 at Tetbury, Gloucs
34 (right) Damaged memorial at Tetbury, Gloucs

dominates the churchyard of Cirencester (Gloucs). Standing on a deep plinth the sarcophagus is raised on large coiled volutes; it has a gadrooned lid and is topped by a flaming urn. Still in Gloucestershire but less pretentious is the unusual monument at Horsley to the Lock family, 1759. On top of a square pedestal a small sarcophagus is set at an angle of 40° and supported on scrolled feet.

6 The Gothic Revival

By the beginning of the nineteenth century, with all the change and upheaval that the Industrial Revolution was to bring, the field of architecture was moving on from the classical to the revival. The Greek Revival at the turn of the century brought a vogue for the *arca* or 'bath-tub' memorial like the one at Wargrave (Berks) with cast iron feet or the elegant one at Purton (Wilts) to Nevil Maskelyn, Astronomer Royal who died in 1811. In the same churchyard is a chest tomb dated 1820 with corner acroteriae, and another at Lea in the same county to the Baker family, 1870. Purton has what must be the best collection of early nineteenth-century memorials in the country, with every possible shape in rich and imaginative variety, many with attractive lettering. At Thursley (Surrey) is a bathtub memorial with a domed piecrust lid and ball finial and *two* feet on each corner. On a memorial at Fairford (Gloucs) to the Harvey family, 1826, are four Egyptian caryatids who appear to be supporting the capping stone with their heads.

Headstones were following the trend of interior wall monuments with weeping figures, urns and sarcophagi in half relief, while other monuments were taking the form of rectangular or tapered Greek *stelae*. In Cumbria and Northumberland headstones were tall and richly decorated, the upper third carved with classical symbolism. The stone to John Peel at Caldbeck, Cumbria, 1854, has delicate foliage flanking the inscription panel; and at Bewcastle (Cumb) there is an impressive group of tall nineteenth-century headstones in red sandstone (35). There is a classical figure on a headstone, 1815, at Arthuret (Nthumb), with the side panels finely decorated with grapes and vine leaves (36); while in the churchyard at Reigate (Surrey) an elegant pyramidion to Baron Masseres, 1825, is carved with a weeping figure in the typical S-shape of Gothic statuary. At Ford (Nthumb) is a beautiful sculpture of two winged angels supporting a heraldic device with a crown and a wreath. It was designed by G F Watts in 1891 and commemorates Louisa, Marchioness of Waterford (37).

By the middle of the nineteenth century a large number of pattern books were in circulation, such as *Designs for Christian Memorials* by John Gibbs, published in 1852, and *Original Designs for Christian Memorials* by Theophilus Smith published in 1864. The designs included crosses, altar-tombs, coped stones, pyramids and shrines in the fast-emerging Gothic style, as well as heraldic devices and alphabets.

In a corner of the tranquil churchyard at Kingscote (Gloucs) is a group of memorials from all periods, commemorating the family of the same name. One of them is a tall Gothic monument with the inscriptions written in indecipherable Gothic lettering on brass scrolls; there is also a shield with the Kingscote family crest hanging from a stone strap.

Throughout the nineteenth century city churchyards were becoming increasingly overcrowded and foul, due largely to the growth of population and consequently burials,

35 Large nineteenth-century headstones at Bewcastle, Cumbria

36 Classical figure on a tall headstone,
1815, at Arthuret,
Northumberland

37 A beautifully sculptured memorial, 1891, at Ford, Northumberland

in urban areas. In the vaults and crypts of urban churches the wealthy in their lead coffins lay forgotten; in the churchyards graves were constantly disturbed to make room for fresh burials.

The development of cemeteries on the rural fringes of cities must have seemed an enormous improvement, laid out as they were like parks, with the memorials in regimented rows between neat paths. The effect on the funeral trade was of double benefit: they meant an increased demand for memorials, while improved transport and communications meant that materials were now available in areas away from where they originated. In addition foreign stones, chiefly marbles, became available with the techniques of mass-production and machine-cut lettering. Throughout the Victorian age and the rise of the 'trade' monumental mason the individual craftsman could no longer compete and the decline of the village mason became inevitable.

The first cemetery to be opened was The Rosary at Norwich, which was licensed in 1819 and was built on five acres of market garden outside the city. Its founder was a non-conformist minister, and because it was not attached to any denominational establishment it was open for burials of dissenters and in fact anyone who could afford to purchase the burial plot.

The great London cemeteries such as Kensal Green and Highgate are a celebration of funerary sculpture. They represent every possible design in a hundred variations: monuments resembling shrines with arches and pinnacles; Egyptian next to Greek, Classic next to Gothic; mausolea side by side with obelisks, marble angels in every possible pose.

By the beginning of the twentieth century much of the inspiration behind the design of churchyard memorials had gone as the rise of the monumental mason was reflected in village churchyards. Headstones of the Gothic window shape (38), marble crosses and open books. The Celtic cross reappeared, often in conjunction with a marble or stone curb filled with green marble chips. Individual craftsmanship became a rarity as the trade

38 A Gothic-Revival headstone, 1887, at Lydney, Gloucs

monumental mason flourished, and churchyard memorials had reached a depressing uniformity.

The most ostentatious churchyard memorial must surely be the one at Reigate (Surrey) to Rebecca Waterlow, who died in 1869. It is fifteen feet long and ten feet high; on the sides are inset panels carved in relief with the Good Samaritan and the Sacrifice of Isaac. On top is a sarcophagus with life-size winged angels seated at either end. It is the work of Samuel Ruddock of Pimlico and totally dominates the churchyard.

The mausoleum

Since prehistoric times, man has buried the dead in tombs, often with grave goods to appease the gods. In England we have thousands of Neolithic tumuli, constructed of massive stones set vertically in the ground to form chambers, with horizontal stones across the top. They were then covered with earth or stones to form a mound. At its most simple, the megalithic burial chamber of prehistory could be described as the first mausoleum, literally a house for the dead.

The mausoleum as we know it today takes its name from Mausolus, ruler of the powerful and wealthy Carian dynasty of Asia Minor in the fourth century BC. His wife Artemesia, who was also his sister, directed the construction of a large and pretentious building in a prominent position above the harbour in the city of Halicarnassus. One of the Seven Wonders of the World, it was later destroyed; it is thought to have been richly decorated with marble columns, carved friezes and tiers of sculpted figures.

The Roman emperor Augustus built an enormous circular mausoleum in Rome in the year 28 BC where his own remains were interred when he died in AD 14. A century later Hadrian built a new imperial mausoleum on the banks of the Tiber, thus establishing the importance of the mausoleum in the history of funerary architecture. Some wealthy Romans even provided communal mausolea known as *columbaria* for relatives and freedmen, possibly similar to those in use in Italy today.

The revival of the classical mausoleum began in the eighteenth century with Castle Howard (Yorks) in 1726; it was also one of the first burials outside consecrated ground. It was followed by others, equally impressive and on private land such as the Yarborough mausoleum at Great Limber (Lincs) and the Royal mausoleum at Frogmore.

In England the Middle Ages were the heyday of the chantry chapel, endowed by the wealthy to ensure a minimal stay in Purgatory. Following the Act of Parliament of 1547 all revenues from chantries were confiscated, and chantry chapels, many of which already contained funerary monuments, were demoted to being the funerary chapels of the families concerned. The Post-Reformation chapels were, with a few exceptions, architecturally unexciting, although the tombs they contained were often highly elaborate, with the deceased in pious attitude surrounded by kneeling figures of the family. One of the best examples is the extended family chapel of the Grey family at Flitton (Beds) which started as a chapel on the north side of the choir and grew over succeeding generations, gaining transepts in all directions. It now contains what must be the best single collection of family monuments in the country. At Melton Constable (Norfk) the Hastings family vault is under the family pew in the south transept, although above ground level, giving the family a pleasantly elevated position among a good collection of wall monuments. The mausoleum at South Carlton (Lincs) was built by Nicholas Stone, whose notebooks have survived and provide interesting details. The Monson memorial has been sadly mistreated, according to legend, by the Puritans. At the other end of the scale is the Styleman mausoleum at Snettisham (Norfk) which is in effect the south transept and is in use as the vestry, complete with toilets.

A number of mausolea, while being almost detached, have access only from the church, like the handsome octagonal mausoleum, 1740, to the Turner family at Kirkleatham (N Yorks). The rather stark mausoleum in the picture-postcard village of Heydon and also the one at Tittleshall (Norfk) are built on to the north side of the chancel but are accessible only from the churchyard.

The first detached churchyard mausolea in England appeared in the mid-seventeenth century with the Bruce mausoleum at Maulden (Beds) built by the first Earl of Elgin in 1656, although later rebuilt, and the small Cabell mausoleum built in the same year at Buckfastleigh (Devon). One of the earliest was the Guise mausoleum in the richly-

endowed churchyard at Elmore (Gloucs), built in 1733 to a Roman design, and thought to be the first building in Europe since Antiquity to use the Roman Doric order without bases. It is described by Samuel Rudder as having a 'pyramidal roof springing at each corner'.[1] Although the pillars still stand, it is now a ruin, a sad loss to the history of the mausoleum in this country **(39)**.

The attractive classical Thompson mausoleum, built in 1760, in the peaceful churchyard at Little Ouseburn (N Yorks), has recently been restored by English Heritage. It has thirteen attached Doric columns with a frieze and cornice surrounding the rotunda beneath a ribbed dome. The undated Jervis mausoleum at Stone (Staffs) thought to be *c*.1760, is another example of mausolea of the Palladian style. At Fawley (Bucks) the Freeman mausoleum of 1750 **(40)**, dominates a small churchyard, which it shares with the Grecian-style Mackenzie mausoleum of a century later.

At Claverton outside Bath (Somset) the mausoleum to Ralph Allen, who died in 1764 is an open square structure with a pyramidal roof and arched sides. The single chest tomb sits in the middle, and it is said that the architect Robert Parsons showed the designs to Allen the day before he died.

The Dashwood mausoleum at West Wycombe (Bucks) is described by Pevsner[2] as 'spectacular and passing strange'. Built in flint, it is perhaps the largest mausoleum constructed in Europe since Antiquity. The enormous hexagonal structure, built in 1764-5 for Sir Francis Dashwood, Lord Le Dispenser, was designed by John Bastard the Younger. It is open to the skies, standing next to the church in a prominent position within a circular hill fort. The three sides to the east are open, with Doric columns under a frieze; those to the west are enclosed and were once used as a columbarium. There are groups of three urns on the angles of the parapet. Inside, a large wall monument with kneeling figures commemorates the two wives of Sir Francis Dashwood; they died in 1710 and 1719, and the monument was brought from the former church. A central urn on a pedestal under an Ionic canopy commemorates Lady Le Despenser, 1769.

40 The Freeman mausoleum, 1750, at Fawley, Bucks

In complete contrast is the little mausoleum to the Streatham family at Chiddingstone (Kent) built in 1735, which has a pyramidal roof with a spiked ball finial and urns on the four corners. Interestingly, it also has ventilation shafts emerging in adjacent false chest tombs

Also outstanding among eighteenth-century mausolea is the memorial to the Hopper family in the little churchyard of Shotley (Northumb). It is all the more surprising because it stands in a small redundant churchyard that is reached by a narrow path. The mausoleum was built in the sixteenth-century Mannerist style and may be the work of an earlier Humphrey Hopper who died in 1663. It has an arched recess holding two recumbent effigies, and above them are two shell-headed niches with formal statues. A scrolled pediment supports two reclining figures and the whole is topped by an arched cupola with pyramid finials. Standing at the top of Greymare Hill, the mausoleum is a landmark for miles around.

The nineteenth century produced the striking Egyptian-style Gillow mausoleum at Thurnham (Lancs), 1830, which has four recessed Egyptian columns on the south side only. In the classical mausoleum to the Earl of Lonsdale at Lowther (Cumb) the second earl sits in solitary splendour on a marble plinth carved with animals. Also in heavy classical style is the stone mausoleum at Chilton Foliat (Wilts) which has thick-set columns on the corners supporting a stone sarcophagus on a plinth.

In the gardens of Bicton Park (Devon) Lady Rolle commissioned Pugin in 1850 to build a mausoleum in memory of her husband John. The mediaeval parish church was largely demolished and part of the east wall rebuilt as the mausoleum. Only the tower and parts of the walls survive from the original church, although mediaeval graffiti can still be seen on the old east wall. Inside the mausoleum, the notable interior has a three-bay wagon roof with delicate carved bosses and a vaulted ceiling with decorative gilded panels.

In addition to the Rolle monument the earlier baroque tomb to Denys Rolle, 1638, has two reclining figures on a chest tomb and a baby lying on the ground.

The Sandys mausoleum in the churchyard at Ombersley (Worcs) is the thirteenth-century chancel of the old church; the side walls are Early English, with nineteenth-century east and west ends and pinnacled buttresses. Just inside the churchyard gates at Englefield Green (Surrey) are the two curious little mausolea built by E B Lamb in about 1860 for the Fitzroy family. One is built in Portland stone, the other in Bath stone, and they both have bands of red brickwork and fish-scale tiles. Inside each is a single chest tomb.

A smaller, domestic version of the mausoleum is the barrel-vaulted oven-tomb found in churchyards around Bethersden (Kent) and at Ruan Lanihorne (Cnwll). They have a distinct resemblance to a modern greenhouse, with a door at one end and shelves inside on which the coffins are laid. In the churchyard at Amesbury (Wilts) is an open tunnel vault under a railed enclosure. The inscription reads:

> This spot should have been the resting place of Edmund Antrobus, Grenadier Guards. He fell at Ypres, Flanders, on October 24, 1914 and lies buried in an orchard at Kruiseik, but no trace of his grave can now be found.

There are currently 230 mausolea on record at the Royal Commission on Historic Monuments, of which a large proportion are in effect extensions of the church with access only from within the church itself. These are listed at the same grade as the church.

The Mausolea and Monuments Trust was established in 1996 with the objectives of assessing the condition of all listed mausolea and encouraging emergency repairs where necessary. The aim is 'that the nation's mausolea will continue to stand in all their sepulchral splendour: not too tidy, but cared for; not in perfect condition, but with their dignity intact.'[3]

Modern churchyard memorials

It wasn't until the Arts and Crafts movement that the feel for change began. Although not directly concerned with churchyard memorials, the movement and its followers, notably Eric Gill, had a far-reaching effect particularly on lettering. He designed the simple headstone at Tolpuddle (Dorset) to James Hammett, who died in 1892 and was the only one of the Tolpuddle Martyrs to return to the village. The stone was erected in 1934 and is an important reminder of one of the major events in the history of the Trade Union movement. Gill's own memorial is a simple inscribed stone at Speen (Bucks).

Architects such as Edwin Lutyens also contributed to churchyard architecture. He designed the classical monument to Thomas Joliffe at Kilmersdon (Somset). It has a simple carving of two figures in relief and very fine lettering **(41)**. Lutyens also designed the inspired lych gate to the same churchyard. Morris himself lies under a memorial designed by Philip Webb at Kelmscot (Oxon). It is a coped slab shaped like a roof, and resembles the wooden graveboards once common in the Home Counties.

41 (left) Modern memorial, 1918, by Lutyens, at Kilmersdon, Somerset
42 (right) Barefoot shepherd, 1901, at Poundstock, Cornwall

Anyone wandering round a modern cemetery or churchyard extension could be forgiven for thinking that mass-produced marble is all that is available to those wishing to erect a memorial to a loved one they have lost. But sometimes, in a quiet corner or discreetly among the more recent burials, a modern headstone is a reminder of the craftsmanship available to those who want something different, something special and above all something individual.

From early this century is the engaging slate at Poundstock (Cnwll) carved with a barefoot shepherd carrying a lamb. It commemorates William Cowling, who died in 1901, and his wife Lydia **(42)**. In the churchyard extension at Pelynt (Cnwll) is a rectangular slate, rough and uncut round the edges and carved with a container of flowers in relief. It is beautifully inscribed to Ann Le Grice, who died in 1990, and the slate has been taken from one of her own pigsties. It is the work of Joe Hemming, who has produced some outstanding work in Cornwall, including a headstone to his own small son **(43)**.

A good example of a modest memorial in Cotswold stone is the one at Swinbrook (Oxon) to the writer and novelist Nancy Mitford (1973) which is a plain rectangle with a

mole, part of the family coat of arms, carved in the head. Her misguided sister Unity is buried in the same churchyard **(Plate 11)**.

A plain headstone stands by the door of the church at Owlpen, near Uley (Gloucs). In the head of the stone is a carved beehive complete with a bronze bee. Michael Lewis, who died in 1984 was a well-known and respected local figure. He was also a beekeeper, and his memorial, which is the work of Bryant Fedden, tells us something about him that relates uniquely to him.

It is now recognised that the planning and erection of a memorial is an important part of the grieving process and of coming to terms with loss. Hand-made memorials (for that is literally what they are) evolve from a long period of mutual discussion and consultation between artist and customer; each is made specifically for that client and the end product is unique. The work of the designer/letter-cutter is aesthetic, not commercial, and the end product is fine craftmanship produced with care and commitment, often in local materials. Because many artists work on their own premises, the cost of a hand-cut stone may not exceed that of the trade counterpart.

The organisation *Memorials by Artists* was set up by Harriet Frazer in 1988 after her family had great difficulty finding someone to create a suitable headstone for her stepdaughter, Sophie. The aims of the organisation are to create a link between people looking for a good memorial and the many fine letter-cutters willing to undertake the

44 Modern ledger to a farmer at Steeple Langford, Wilts

work. They also have a wider aim to create an interest in memorial art as a whole, and to encourage new lettering artists. Sophie's headstone, carved by Simon Verity in Salle churchyard (Norfk) is a memorial in the most literal sense to the work of Harriet Frazer.

All over the country there is a rich variety of fine modern work. At Aldeburgh (Suffk) are a number of memorials to musicians, including Benjamin Britten and Joan Cross, described as 'a rare singer.' Nearby a stone to Beth Welford is carved with gardening tools. Also in Suffolk by the thatched church of Thornham Parva is a beautiful slate headstone to David Martin, violinist, **(Plate 12)** and a small slate in the ground to Fredericke Grinke, also a violinist. In complete contrast are two plain raised ledgers with a minimal inscription to Basil Spence, architect of Coventry Cathedral, and his wife.

On the stone to David Talbot Rice at Coln Rogers (Gloucs) agricultural tools and a bull are carved with the inscription 'byzantine scholar and much-loved countryman'. At Steeple Langford (Wilts) a modern ledger commemorating a farmer is carved in relief with a single sheaf of wheat **(44)**.

The Verity workshops have produced some superb work; in the churchyard at Rodbourne (Wilts) are stones of intricate detail, one with a relief carving of a man with his team of horses, ploughing. Most impressive of all is Simon Verity's grand monument in Cotswold stone to the Duke of Beaufort in the small churchyard at Badminton House (Gloucs), where old headstones are set into the churchyard wall. On top of a large chest tomb base a crown sits on a tasselled cushion. Beneath a moulded edge is a portcullis above the family coat of arms. On one side of it is a lion rampant and on the other a tubby dragon with bulging eyelids, the family motto draped between them. Against the backdrop of Badminton Park this memorial by Simon Verity in palest Cotswold stone is an impressive sight **(Plate 13)**.

By contrast the slate headstone at Clyffe Pypard (Wilts) to Nikolaus Pevsner and his

45 Plain headstone to Nikolaus Pevsner and his wife at Clyffe Pypard, Wilts

wife Lola is plain to the point of austerity. For a man who spoke with dry humour of the excesses of British architecture perhaps this is entirely suitable **(45).** In the same vein the group of slate memorials at Grasmere (Cumb) to the Wordsworth family sits happily in a tranquil churchyard among the surrounding hills.

Nearly every churchyard has one or two memorials to those who gave their lives for 'our tomorrows.' In counties such as Wiltshire where there are strong associations with the Forces, the silent serried ranks of identical stones are a moving reminder of the horrors of war. Military aircraft still climb over the churchyards of Lyneham, Wroughton, Fovant and many more where more recent conflicts have added to the memorials. In the churchyard at Sherston is the restored military memorial to George Strong VC, who died in 1888. He won the Victoria Cross for an act of bravery in the Crimean War at the age of 21, and was one of the earliest recipients of the award. In the south of the county at Semley is a bronze statue of a soldier in a tropical helmet on a horse. It commemorates the death in 1915 of Lieutenant George Dewrance Irving Armstrong of the Sherwood Foresters.

Monuments eccentric and unusual

It is part of the unpredictability of being a churchyard enthusiast that now and again one comes upon something totally unexpected; it may be an aberration or a folly, but it provides an insight into the eccentricities of the mason or his client. Until recently there was little control over churchyard monuments, and people who felt that an elaborate or unconventional memorial was a desirable indication of wealth or status were not bound by restrictions. In the churchyard at Barnes, Greater London, is an extraordinary stone

46 Memorial to those killed building a railway tunnel, Otley, W Yorks

tent in which lie the remains of the explorer Sir Richard Burton and his wife Isabella. Erected in 1891, the tent is made of Forest of Dean stone, carved to look like canvas and is so realistic that it comes as a surprise to find it is solid.

During his lifetime a Sussex squire known as 'Mad Jack' had a 20ft pyramid built for himself in the churchyard at Brightling. When he died in 1833 legend had it that he was buried sitting up in full evening dress with a top hat, and that he had buried with him a roast chicken and a bottle of claret, presumably for his journey to the hereafter. Since he is said to have weighed twenty-two stone the picture defies belief, and the story has since been discredited.

In better taste is the monument in the churchyard at Otley (W Yorks) which commemorates the men killed during the construction of the Bramhope railway tunnel during the years 1845-9. It is a castellated model of a tunnel with towers on the four corners and is in superb condition **(46)**.

More modest in scale is the attractive monument at Offton (Suffk) to John Wyatt who died in 1867. On top of an unremarkable domed chest tomb is the figure of the deceased beneath his shroud while his daughter leads his horse to mourn over its master. This is a delightful and unusual memorial, sensitively executed.

Cornwall is rich in oddities, of which the grandest is the baroque memorial at Probus to Sir Christopher Hawkins, who died in 1829. The chest tomb has elaborately decorated cartouches flanked by corner posts with fleur-de-lys capitals. The lid is supported on each corner by an almost life-size kneeling figure wearing seventeenth-century armour. This

47 Unusual monument to Sir Christopher Hawkins, 1829, at Probus, Cornwall

striking memorial is the only one of its type in the country **(47)**.

In the churchyard at Madron, almost dwarfing the Greek-style mausoleum in the same churchyard, is an enormous memorial to John Scobell Armstrong (d 1929). On top of it, sitting on a huge granite sphere is the copper figure of a blindfold maiden plucking at a lyre with a broken string. Underneath are the lines:

> A broken string and through the drift
> Of aeons sad with human cries
> She waits the Hand of God to lift
> The bandage from her eyes.

There is another bronze sculpture of a youth playing a harp at Stratton.

In the churchyard at Felling (T & W) is a 'four-poster' memorial to the Haddon family, dated 1717. It has three recumbent figures in contemporary dress lying under a decorated quilt, with inscribed oval panels on the headboard and a coat of arms on the reverse.

At Richmond (N Yorks) is the plain ledger to a merchant, Robert Willance, the inscription still legible. It is said that in 1606 he fell two hundred feet on horseback and survived at the cost of an amputated leg, which he had buried and commemorated by a stone. On his death ten years later he and the leg were re-united under one memorial.

High in the Oxfordshire Cotswolds at Idbury, a small churchyard rich in wildlife surrounds a Norman church. Not only does it boast a large polished marble heart, but also a strange monument on four curved legs that looks more like a landing craft on the moon than a churchyard memorial. It commemorates Sir Benjamin Baker KCB, KCMG, FRS, titled 'King of the Steel Age' and designer of the Forth Bridge, who died in 1907. The family have evidently moved away, as the monument is overgrown.

But the oddest memorial of all, which is not a memorial at all in the strictest sense, must be that to William Tinney of Crantock (Cnwll), the last man to be held in the stocks and 'a smuggler and a vagabond.' He is depicted on a carved panel outside the church, sitting with his feet in the stocks and his arms folded, a feather in his hat. The wall plaque records how he 'robbed a widow woman with violence' in 1817, and was put in the stocks to await justice. He managed to escape, lowered himself from the church tower using the rope from the tenor bell and according to the adjacent plaque, 'in the view of certain village worthies bolted, got off to sea and was never brought to justice or seen in the neighbourhood again'. The stocks survive, bleached silver with age.

7 Sculpture, symbolism and imagery

.

In his article 'Rude Forefathers', on the headstones of Kent and Sussex, Innes Hart writes:

> Three things seem to be necessary before fine original work can be produced. There must be good local stone; there must be a fine tradition of craftsmanship and pattern-making; and here and there must be individual craftsmen with a personal and inventive sense of beauty, or else with the rarer faculty of expressing thought and emotion in stone.[1]

These sentiments describe absolutely the traditions behind much of our finest churchyard work. The churchyard memorial is not only an artefact, it is marker for the burial site, a record of the deceased and a statement of faith in the concepts of mortality and resurrection. The representation of these concepts in churchyard sculpture follows the vagaries of fashion and finance over succeeding generations, often with humour and sentimentality. For hundreds of years the changes in British architecture and design have been mirrored in the mason's yard, with the individual craftsman producing his own interpretation according to the restrictions of space and material and the desires of the client. The vast majority of this work would have been carried out by local craftsmen incorporating their own interpretations of the symbols of death and resurrection together with the imagery of the Bible. We only have to look at the Gothic splendour of some of our great cathedrals, at the intricate and humorous detail of the church at Kilpeck (Herefs) and indeed at almost any parish church to find sculpture that is surely inspirational in its skill and representation. Much of the architectural element of late eighteenth-century memorials can be related to the building of grand houses all over the country as well as to ecclesiastical design, as we have already seen in the lyre-console. The scrolled cartouche of the Georgian era was another feature often found in domestic architecture; a pedestal tomb at Marden (Herefs) decorated with a ball-flower ornament is an interesting Gothic revival rarely seen on a Victorian monument.

The other major sources of design were the pattern books of the seventeenth and eighteenth centuries of craftsmen such as William Halfpenny and Batty Langley. From Francis Quarles' *Hieroglyphics of the Life of Man* (1639) comes the image of Death with a dart seen on a number of headstones including a graphic one at Ardingly (Sussex)[2] **(Plate 14)**.

The eighteenth-century furniture trade was another rich source of design; individual elements such as lozenges and bosses appear on early monuments like those at South Wraxall (Wilts) and Upton St Leonards (Gloucs). Sequential designs such as guilloche can be found in the Forest of Dean while the pie-crust effect of gadrooning is a common and

48 Headstone following furniture design, 1823, Stratton, Cornwall

dramatic feature of many of the finest Cotswold monuments. A number of slate ledgers, particularly the rich collections of Morley and Lightcliffe (W Yorks) have decorative hearts and scrolls which can be found on seventeenth-century chair-backs and occasionally the outline of the chair-back is mimicked by the shape of the headstone, as on the unusual headstone at Stratton (Cnwll), 1823 **(48)**. A number of slate headstones at Swithland (Leics) and the surrounding churchyards have arched surrounds and highly decorative capitals of ornamental woodwork seen on chests and chair-backs of the Jacobean period [3]. A striking example among the slate headstones at Egloshayle (Cnwll) has reeded columns and Corinthian capitals flanking a finely decorated arch and keystone. It is the work of Robert Oliver and commemorates James Hawke, who died in 1827.

All over the country the work characteristic of the individual craftsman can often be traced to a particular area. The mason of the seventeenth and early eighteenth century brought his own skills and imagination to each piece of work, and his own, perhaps limited, knowledge and symbolism. The majority of early memorials incorporate the skull, the ultimate representation of death and a reminder of the mortality to which we must all succumb. There is a noticeable difference between the rustic slates of Cornwall and Devon and the sophistication of the Midlands. On the slates of Cornwall they often have an attractive naiveté and simplicity, the outline incised, with the eyes cut as deep sockets and the teeth much in evidence. There is a gruesome one at St Veryan with the lower jaw missing; a skull and crossbones at Botus Fleming records M Brown who died in 1734/5. This confusion about dates is not uncommon, and may have something to do

49 Skull and crossbones, Botus Fleming, Cornwall. Note confusion about date

with the change from the Julian to the Gregorian calendar which did not become law until the Calendar (New Style) Act of 1751 **(49)**.

Regional variations in design depend on the availability of suitable materials and the craftsman's access to sources of design, as well as on social and economic factors. The limestone belt which created the great 'wool' wealth and some of our most notable churches also provided an endless supply of high-quality stone and attracted some of the best masons. The Wiltshire limestone seems to have lent itself to particularly fine relief carving; on a late eighteenth century tomb at Hullavington the central panel has an oval cartouche surrounded by egg and dart moulding with cherub heads in the spandrels. The pilasters on either side are finely and delicately carved with flowers and foliage in relief **(50)**. There are similar memorials at Castle Combe, Corsham, Potterne and several others. A slight variation occurs where the inscription panels are carved with shield shapes; some of the best are in the secluded churchyard of Langley Burrell, where Parson Kilvert was curate to his father. The description he wrote in his *Diary* on the first Sunday in May 1871 could still apply today:

> I went into the churchyard under the feathering larch which sweeps over the gate. The ivy-grown old church with its noble tower stood beautiful and silent among the elms with its graves at its feet. Everything was still. No-one was about or moving and the only sound was the singing of birds. The place was all in a charm of singing, full of peace and quiet sunshine. It seemed to be given up to the birds and their morning hymns. It was the bird church, the church among the birds. I wandered round the church among the dewy grass-grown

50 Fine carving on a chest tomb, 1797, at Hullavington, Wilts

graves and picturesque ivy and moss hung tombstones. Round one grave grew a bed of primroses. Upon another tall cowslips hung their heads.

In a few churchyards in north Gloucestershire are headstones carved with little figures in pantaloons carrying palms, as though the mason had chosen to depict some Eastern influence. Palm branches are traditionally carried at Easter, and are symbolic of victory over death. On the Gloucestershire/Herefordshire border near Newent are headstones carved with bunches of grapes, in an area where there are vineyards to this day. At Standish (Gloucs) the beautiful Niblett tomb, 1676, has two laid-back weepers sitting on toothy skulls; beneath the swag of fruits and flowers is a crayfish, a reminder that at one time freshwater shellfish were found in the River Severn **(Plate 15)**. The Fruits of the Earth are lavishly represented on many Cotswold tombs, at a time when similar symbolism was appearing in art and poetry. In the small churchyard of Churcham (Gloucs) is a chest tomb, 1784, with a pineapple carved in half relief, a very early use of exotic fruit.

In two churchyards close together in south Somerset are similar chest tombs carved with caryatids. The earlier one at Broomfield, 1653, has a deep frieze with paterae and grotesque masks; the later one at West Monkton has an ornate frieze with lions' masks, rosettes and lozenges. The date is illegible, but is recorded as 1683 or 1688.

In Kent the outline of the head of the stone is occupied by a skull like the one with a human face and haunted eyes at Plaxtol. Where the stone is a 'double' the second head is often filled with crossed bones. On a chest tomb at Wisbech St Mary (Cambs) is a deep-eyed skull with its chin resting on the other symbol of mortality, the hourglass. Sometimes the skull or the hourglass are winged; on a headstone at Littledean (Gloucs) is an hourglass with one wing of a bird, representing day, the other that of a bat representing night. In Kent the early eighteenth-century hourglass is treated with a engaging frivolity, in the shape of a double heart or a figure of eight. On one of the restored headstones in the mason's yard at Great Bedwyn (Wilts) is a central winged hourglass flanked by frowning skulls. Sticking out behind them are the heads of a pick and shovel, tools of the sexton, which may have represented the trade of the deceased. At Lower Wraxall (Dorset) a chest tomb with rounded ends has skulls in three-quarters relief on one end and a coat-of-arms on the other; it commemorates Francis Bennett who died in 1728.

An important and attractive stone at Broadway (Worcs) is in danger of sinking. It shows the figure of the deceased in period costume kneeling before Death, with a strange representation of an angel's head and what could be a wheel or a flower **(Plate 16)**.

The symbolic representation of the figure of Death is found on a number of slate headstones, usually as part of a deathbed scene. On a headstone at Thurlow (Suffk) is the dramatic scene of Death standing over a swaddled mother and baby while a third figure tries to fight him off **(51)**. At St Margaret's, Leicester, the figure of Death with his dart offers a dying man a globe, taunting him with the pleasures of the world. In the same sculpture is a clock, representing the passage of time, which is found occasionally on slates, but rarely on stone, presumably because of the fine carving required. A similar scene on a slate headstone at Sherington (Bucks) has not only the clock but also Father Time in dramatic posture. At St Mary de Castro, Leicester is a powerful sculpture of Father Time among the clouds with a very workmanlike scythe; it commemorates Samuel Bankart who died in 1799.

In the churchyard of Broadwoodwidger (Devon) is the delightful slate commemorating Thomas Palmer, who died in 1789. It has three scenes in the head of the stone. In the centre the skeleton of Death with his dart holds back the curtain of the death bed, where the dying man, already in the rigid pose of the dead, has 'Welcome Death' on a scroll emerging from his mouth. Above his bed the angels of resurrection wait. The scenes on either side show angels consoling the grieving parents with pious messages on scrolls. Above the central plaque a clock shows the inevitability of time with the moral message: 'Let every youth prepared be, least Death should strike so young as me.' At the bottom of the stone is the descriptive epitaph:

> Just in my youthful blooming age
> God took me from this earthly stage.
> It was by a putrid fever sore
> Not long when seiz'd before I was no more.

The theme of resurrection is usually represented by angels or by the cherub-head, thought symbolically to be the soul of the deceased winging its way to heaven. Both can be seen in almost every churchyard, in the spandrels of chest tomb panels, on headstones in every shape and form. In the Cotswolds winged cherubs occupy the head of the stone, often

51 Death threatens a mother and child, 1797 Thurlow, Suffolk

with their fingers holding a book which represents the Bible. On a headstone at Longney (Gloucs) there is a central head which may be a portrait, with cavorting cherubs on either side looking as though they are pulling her hair. At Fairford a row of Georgian headstones have multiple heads, in one case as many as four.

The cherub or angel heads of Kent come in a variety of designs, sometimes in profile and with an interesting selection of headgear. A stone at East Peckham to William Austin (d 1754) and his wife has on one side a head in profile with a headband and wispy curls of hair, and on the other a diagrammatic pair of crossed bones. There is a similar one with a strange head-dress at West Peckham to the Buttenshaw family, 1756, which must surely be the work of the same man.

On a chest tomb at Ashton Keynes (Wilts) two clerical-looking figures are holding up a curtain, their feet peeping out underneath. Cherubs are peeking coyly round the corner of the volute, and on the side panels there are no less than three. At Amesbury cherubs share the headstone with a skull and crossbones, while at Hullavington (Wilts) two full-length cherubs are whispering together as though sharing a secret **(52)**. The two cherubs on the end of a chest tomb at Godmanstone (Dorset) are actually kissing.

During the course of the eighteenth century the cherub head developed into the full-length figure, as masons produced their own interpretations of classical art. The trumpeting angels of salvation can be seen flying across the headstones of Cornwall, and at All Saints, Leicester a pair of athletic and well-bosomed angels are vigorously blowing their trumpets. On a headstone at Trowbridge (Wilts) two scantily clad angels with trumpets tucked under their arms are supporting a book, while the eye of God looks down from above. There is an almost identical stone at Stourton (Wilts).

*52 Two cherubs with a secret,
Hullavington, Wilts*

At St Breock (Cnwll), where a stream runs through the churchyard and the birdsong is deafening, is a headstone to Richard Blake, who died in 1848, with a figure in a loose dress unmistakably waving farewell, like a child going off to school. There is also a slate, 1761, to Richard Lobb with a skeleton and pierced hearts in the spandrels and the legend: Death with his dart hath pierced his heart.

The calligraphic slate angels on the headstones of Cornwall, with their angel-mop hair and surprised expressions, have an individuality and an appeal which is unique to the area. Some have wings growing from their ears, others have them spreading out under the chin like inflated shoulder-pads. Every churchyard will have one or two; Cardinham has several; one at Lanivet has two dissimilar angels on the same stone and records two little girls who died within a month of each other in 1782. Underneath like a child's drawing is the top half of a skeleton with skinny arms holding an hourglass and a dart.

The most common classical symbol, seen in every churchyard and cemetery until the end of the Victorian era is the funerary urn, which occurs in every possible shape and form from modest inscribed headstones to three-dimensional sculptures topping pedestals and obelisks. They are often draped or wreathed in foliage and are at their most elegant on the late eighteenth-century slates of the Midlands.

The tree often appears in conjunction with the urn or sarcophagus and frequently with mourning figures or weepers. Together they present a classic image of grief, its variations appearing in every churchyard. There are several in among the superb collection of early nineteenth-century stones at Portland (Dorset); on one the foliage of a skilfully carved tree follows the curve of the stone, and a weeper in a tight-waisted dress holds her hand to her head.

53 Symbols of mortality on a stone at Burgh, Suffolk

The shell or scallop has been used as an architectural feature since Roman times. In the Middle Ages it was adopted as the badge of the Christian pilgrim. On a chest tomb at Stanton St Quentin (Wilts) an enormous scallop shell supported by acanthus scrolls occupies the whole of the end panel. On Cotswold 'bale' tombs the concave ends of the bale stone lend themselves to the shell form, sometimes in conjunction with a skull or ram's head.

The serpent, usually coiled in a circle biting its own tail, is a classic symbol of eternity. There is a typical one on a small headstone at Burgh (Suffk) surrounded by a coffin and sexton's tools **(53)**. Among a group of nineteenth-century slates at Penshurst (Kent) are two with serpents and two with the symbolism of the sickle and the cut flower, indicating life cut down in its prime **(Plate 17)**. At Saul (Gloucs) on a stone to a ship's carpenter it appears sampling the fruit from an unlikely-looking apple tree in a scene that includes a draped urn and bears no relationship to the Garden of Eden.

The book, apart from its obvious interpretation as the Bible, could also be the prayer book or the book of knowledge. It frequently appears on Cotswold memorials, just under the angel's chin, with the fingers holding it from above. On a stone at Hadlow (Kent) dated 1782 two chaste-looking maidens are engaged in devotional studies in a scene that would not be out of place in a Jane Austen novel.

Other forms of symbolism include the broken column, another representation of life cut short at Lacock **(54)**, Nettleton and St Mark's, Swindon (Wilts); the falling building or tower which may indicate pride, is at Stanstead (Suffk) and Arlingham (Gloucs) and occurs on several headstones in Kent. The tree when growing represents Life, when fallen, Death and appears several times in the Severn Vale in John Pearce's 'cauliflower' form

54 Symbolism of a broken column, Lacock, Wilts

with a weeper sitting underneath. On the pair of Morgan tombs, 1697, at Fairford (Gloucs) is a rare depiction of a mirror, which in the Middle Ages was seen as the mirror of conscience (1 Corinthians 13:12), in association with books, trumpets, an hourglass and a serpent, and foliage emerging from a skull. If this is a Green Man (see p.30), pagan symbolism is rare outside the church although there is one on the end of a chest tomb at Slimbridge and another in the neighbouring parish of Coaley (Gloucs).

In the churchyard at Mitford (Nthumb) is a nineteenth-century headstone to several members of the Walker family, including one who had returned from Jamaica. The imagery of the stone is unclear: the carving shows a well-endowed female figure with an angel to one side, and on the other a man carrying some sort of stave or pole with a cross-bar at the top. It does not appear to be a biblical image although on either side is the conventional symbolism of serpent, dart and hourglass **(55)**.

Flowers are very much part of our funeral culture, although formal floral tributes did not appear until the late 1860s. The churchyards of the Forest of Dean (Gloucs) are particularly rich in symbolic carving, much of it in mint condition. Several have small late seventeenth- and early eighteenth-century headstones carved in a design that can only be described as folk art, with stylised flowers and foliage and rounded symmetrical heads. Two neighbouring stones at Littledean demonstrate the change in design in as little as 40 years: William Rock, who died in 1710, has an 'ear-muff' hood to the stone with stylised flowers and leaves, and underneath a circular cartouche with a decorated frame **(Plate 18)**. The stone to John Reynolds, 1740, who was one of 'ye keepers of ye Forest of Dean' has a plain hood to the stone and naturalised flowers carved in relief. There is no cartouche; the inscription is carved on the face of the stone. Similar stones can be found at Newland and Awre. Lydney has an assortment of cherub-heads, many with wings; a

1   *The Hopper mausoleum at Shotley, Northumb.*

2   *The approach to St Just-in-Roseland, Cornwall*

3   *The Bewcastle cross, Cumbria*

4   *Celtic cross at Cardinham, Cornwall*

5   *Anthropomorphic headstone at East Peckham, Kent*

6 *Lettering on a ledger at Lightcliffe, W Yorks*

7 *The Ricardo monument, 1823, at Hardenhuish, Wilts*

8   *Memorial to Valentine Strong, Master Mason, at Fairford, Gloucs*

9   *Lyre-ended chest tomb to William Atkyns, 1670, at Upton St Leonards, Gloucs*

10   *Squires monument, 1781, at Burton Lazars, Leics*

11   *Nancy Mitford's headstone at Swinbrook, Oxon*

12   *Modern headstone at Thornham Parva, Suffolk*

13 *The Beaufort memorial at Badminton, Gloucs*

14   *Death with his dart on a headstone at Ardingley, Sussex*

15   *Detail of the*
      Niblett memorial,
      1676, at
      Standish, Gloucs

16   *The deceased kneels before Death, 1685, at Broadway, Worcs*

17   *Symbolism of the broken stem on a slate at Penshurst, Kent*

18   Folk art on William Rock's headstone, 1710, at Littledean, Gloucs

19   *The Knowles chest tomb, 1707, at Elmore, Gloucs*

20   *Headstone to Ann Holmes and her daughter, 1796, at Desborough, Northants*

21   Enigmatic headstone, 1798, at
       Thornbury, Gloucs

22   The Flight into Egypt on a headstone at Pembury, Kent

23   *Farmer Perrott, killed by his flail, Upper Cam, Gloucs*

24   *Chest tomb to Robert Hopper, 1725, at Barnard Castle, Durham*

25   *Roman lettering on a headstone at Awre, Gloucs*

55 Unusual imagery on a headstone at Mitford. Northumberland52

stone to Elizabeth Evans has a cherub in a tight-fitting bonnet with the wings coming out by her ears and forming the top of the stone. A double headstone, 1787, has two panels separated by husk drops with tassels and drapes. The two heads have their central wings raised and crossed; there is apparently no symbolic significance to this, it is simply the configuration of the stone. An odd and unique stone at Newnham is carved with no less than thirteen heads, with a delicate tracery of angels' wings in the background. Two of the heads are large, the rest represent children. The enigmatic inscription records 'Susannah wife of James Drew who died February 10th 1796 aged 41 yeares (sic). Also two of their children Phoebe and Emmanuel, and nine of their sons of Susan's parents'.

The development of the cherub-head into the full-length figure can be seen here too: at Lydney (Gloucs) are two stones with buxom trumpet-blowing angels in curious head-dresses, their lower bodies tastefully concealed by cornucopia and acanthus leaves. Another, 1788, has an angel carved in relief rising from a bed of clouds. She has diminutive wings with a trumpet in her left hand and a scroll in her right, all carved in relief.

While headstones allowed only a limited area for sculpture, the chest tomb presents four panels for decoration; at the same time the overhang of the ledger provides a certain amount of protection against the weather. A chest tomb at Standish (Gloucs) has the end panels deeply carved with the figure of a small boy kneeling at a *prie-dieu*. Over his head is a shelf, the symbolic division between this world and the next, and above that a bearded Father Time with his hourglass and scythe. On a chest tomb at Tibberton (Gloucs), dated 1755 Father Time is a strange figure wearing a loincloth and gripping an hourglass in his hand as though his life depended on it. He has an odd stance, looking as though he has dislocated shoulders, and this is typical of the work of Giles Samson.

In the small village of Elmore (Gloucs), almost on the banks of the River Severn, is one of the richest churchyards in an area that is particularly well-endowed. Here the Grade II★ Knowles chest tomb, 1707, must be the most magnificent memorial in the country. The south side has all the figures of symbolism: a winged Father Time on the left, with his hourglass and scythe, stands on a wheel, for eternity; to the right a skeleton is standing on an globe, for mortality. The central roundel has an open book above with two figures in long robes holding it on either side. The left-hand figure has a realistically carved shoe showing below his robe. Between the end figures and the central pair are two plump angels blowing trumpets into the ears of the others. On either side of the roundel at the bottom of the panel are two children, each holding a book and sitting on skulls which are expertly foreshortened, a skilled piece of technical carving.

The north panel also has a circular roundel but with only the four main figures, of which the skeleton has largely disappeared. The lyre ends are also deeply carved with deep acanthus scrolls, the east with a heart-shaped cartouche, the west with an elaborate heraldic plaque and beneath it a small panel containing a recumbent lion. The skill and organisation of this memorial is outstanding in early eighteenth-century sculpture **(Plate 19)**.

Often, as we have seen with the skeleton of Death in the bedchamber, symbolism appears in conjunction with pictorial imagery. But death is also represented by direct imagery — figures of the dead, coffins, sexton's tools. In the churchyard at Standish (Gloucs) is a unique chest tomb carved with the figures of two men. They are sitting up, holding hands with the Book between them, their feet on a skull. They were evidently men of substance, because they are wearing full-bottomed wigs, and yet they are dressed in their winding sheets as though ready for burial. The adjacent memorial has a single standing figure similarly dressed; they commemorate the Halling family, who died in 1680 and 1735 respectively, in an unusual and interesting depiction.

More poignant is the headstone at Desborough (Hants) to Anne Holmes and her daughter Harriet who lie side by side on a finely carved slate, the child in the crook of her mother's arm **(Plate 20)**. Less skilful but equally engaging is the headstone at Portland (Dorset) to Grace Comben and her two daughters who died in childbirth in 1775. They are depicted together in a four-poster bed with an angel tastefully holding back the curtain **(56)**.

On a most unusual headstone at Thornbury (Gloucs) is a portrait figure of a woman with her torso shown as a laurel wreath on a pedestal. Beneath pendulous breasts is the head of a child, and the imagery perhaps indicates that the mother and child died with the child *in utero* **(Plate 21)**. Death is graphically represented by the open, occupied coffin on a headstone at Speldhurst (Kent). At Fairford and Southrop (Gloucs) diminutive stone coffins complete with handles sit on top of chest tombs.

Towards the end of the eighteenth century the depiction of the three Pauline virtues of the Christian life — Faith, Hope and Charity were beginning to appear. Faith is represented by some of the apocalyptic imagery on the slates of Leicester and Swithland (Leics). At St Margaret's, Leicester a slate to Robert Denshire, 1761, death is depicted by the corpse centrally in a coffin. To the left is a graveyard of crumbling tombs with a skull, a serpent

56 Mother and two daughters who died in childbirth, 1775, Portland, Dorset

and a withered tree; to the right a cross and chalice and a resurrected tree surrounded by rays of glory and heavenly souls. It is a skilled and intricately carved piece of imagery. In the same churchyard a large chest tomb has the apocalypse on one side and the resurrection on the other.

The figure of Hope with her anchor is more common and features in a large number of churchyards. There is a draped figure with an outsize anchor among the superb collection at St Mary de Castro, Leicester to Ann and William Dowse, 1790; and a neat figure on a stone at Arlingham (Gloucs) with an upturned boat **(57)**. In the neighbouring churchyard of Saul is the Victorian interpretation of the anchor in white marble set against a pile of rocks, commonly found in coastal churchyards.

Charity is often represented as the heart, and appears on a number of seventeenth-century headstones including several Cornish slates. The figure of Charity shown as a mother nursing her children is beautifully depicted on a slate at Burton Lazars (Leics) to Mary Blower, 1781, with an identical one at All Saints, Leicester.

Biblical scenes feature mainly in two areas: West Kent and the Vale of Evesham. In Kent they are all on headstones of similar outline; the best survivals are at Capel, Plaxtol and West Peckham. At Plaxtol a stone with a scrolled surround depicts the Flight into Egypt, with the figures of Joseph, Mary and the Christ Child followed by a mule, and a winged angel showing them the way. It commemorates William Broad who died in 1774. There is a similar representation at Capel and also under a tree at Pembury, where Mary is riding the mule, the Christ Child in her arms **(Plate 22)**. At Hadlow a stone to Henry Kipping, who died in 1784, with a plainer surround represents the *Noli Me Tangere* (Touch Me Not)

57 Hope with her Anchor at Arlingham, Gloucs

scene, where Mary mistakes Christ for the gardener by giving Him a spade. On either side the other two Marys wait in front of a church, while in the background the two remaining crosses lie on the ground, with Jerusalem in the top corner. Other Biblical scenes include the Resurrection at Capel, where a female figure rises from a sarcophagus while Time breaks his dart across his knee; there is a similar one at Plaxtol, where a collapsing tower in is danger of falling on her head. The Good Samaritan is at Capel and Speldhurst and a well-preserved stone at East Peckham to Ann Long (d 1779) shows the Agony in the Garden with Christ holding a cross and the buildings of Jerusalem again in the background.

The Garden of Eden can be found on an eighteenth-century stone at Portland (Dorset), where the serpent is entwined in the tree and two cherubs hold a book at arms' length in the foreground as though disassociating themselves from the scene above. At Stanstead (Suffk) an allegorical headstone shows a church and churchyard on one side and on the other a weeping willow and an urn. In between is a trumpeting angel complete with scroll, in a horizontal image of the resurrection.

In the Vale of Evesham a group of churchyards have large thin stones depicting a variety of Biblical scenes in fine detail, often with the fruits and flowers of the region in the surround. Unfortunately many of these are in poor condition, but two of the best survivals are the pair of slates at Dumbleton (Gloucs), said to be the work of Samuel Hobbs. They commemorate Richard Clayton and his wife Hester (d 1797 and 1792) and are carved with biblical scenes. One is of the Crucifixion, a rarity in churchyard imagery: there is one on an early rustic stone at Lydney (Gloucs) and another in the bale-end of a modern chest tomb at Burford (Oxon).

A further category of churchyard imagery can only be described as biographical, where the memorial depicts the life or even the death of the deceased. A headstone at Thursley (Surrey) known as the Sailor's Stone has a graphic carving in relief of the unfortunate victim being attacked. His murderers were later hanged on Gibbet Hill, Hindhead in chains made at Thursley Forge.

A chest tomb at Upper Cam (Gloucs) has a relief carving said to be that of Farmer Perrott in period costume with his plough. The legend has it that the loose length of chain — clearly visible — decapitated him *because he was ploughing on a Sunday*. **(Plate 23)** At Westbury-on-Severn (Gloucs) is a beautiful portrait of schoolmaster William Clarke, who died in 1835. He is shown sitting at his desk in a wide-skirted coat and breeches, writing with a quill pen. Around him are artist's and draughtsman's tools, showing him to be a man of many talents. Another stone at Broadway (Worcs) commemorates William Haslam, who died in 1786 and was a barber. His headstone has a central cherub-head surrounded by scissors, comb and razor.

At Littledean (Gloucs) is a six-foot-tall headstone with a full-length portrait in low relief of a small boy in breeches and boots. The date and the inscription is lost, apart from a few words of 'Suffer Little children ...' Who was he, and who grieved for him?

Not surprisingly for a maritime nation, shipwrecks are often represented in churchyard sculpture. There is a famous one at Bosham (Hants) showing a small figure falling overboard. Another at Mylor (Cnwll) shows a small ship amid towering waves, the inscription commemorates the 'Warriors, women and children who on their return to England from the Coast of Spain unhappily perished in the Wreck of the Queen Transport on Trefusis Point, January 14, 1814'. The west country is not short of shipwreck memorials: there is a large monument at Brixham (Devon) and several at St Keverne and Saltash. In the cliff-top churchyard of Morwenstow, so admirably recorded by poet-parson Robert Stephen Hawker, vicar of Morwenstow 1834-35, in his book *Footprints of Former Men in Cornwall*, he describes how he and his parishioners buried between thirty and forty shipwrecked seamen, the crews of three lost vessels, in unmarked graves beneath the trees along the southern side of the churchyard. Nearby the painted figurehead of the *Caledonia* stands over the graves of her crew.

Several of the villages that border the treacherous lower reaches of the River Severn in Gloucestershire have memorials recording master mariners, ships carpenters, and little boys who drowned in the 'Bristol River,' a reminder that at one time many of these riverside communities were ports. At Newnham is another graphic carving of a shipwreck with the dinghy overturned and a helpless figure standing in the bow; it has a long epitaph recording the deaths of two young men in 1848. On a chest tomb at Arlingham is a beautiful carving of a sinking ship in memory of Frederick Longney who died at the age of 15 in 1819. Many of the names at Arlingham also occur at Newnham, also a reminder that not long ago a ferry linked these two communities.

Finally, a not insignificant part of churchyard sculpture is concerned with heraldry. Heraldic emblems, while only a shadow of their counterparts inside the church, are an important and integral part of many of our finest monuments, such as the Beaufort tomb at Badminton (see p 83) and the Knowles tomb at Elmore (Gloucs) (see p 98). At Barnard

58 Detailed heraldic imagery on a chest tomb at Beaconsfield, Bucks

Castle (Dur) the chest tomb to Robert Hopper, who died in 1725 aged 23, stands in a prominent position on corner piers close to the church wall and is richly carved. On the north side is a gentleman dressed in detailed early eighteenth-century costume with sidecoat and hat. On the south side a skeleton with scythe, and on a side panel two trumpeting cherubs clasping a crown above a Book quoting Revelations Chapter II v 10: '...be thou faithful unto death, and I will give thee a crown of life'. The left-hand panel has a coat of arms flanked by flowers, all in excellent condition. The ledger above has a prominent overhang which will have protected the side panels; it has a moulding of acanthus leaves carved with cherub-heads on top **(Plate 24)**.

A number of Cotswold chest tombs have coats of arms, with the best at Bourton-on-the Water, Burford, Painswick and Standish. Ledgers are often carved with striking heraldry, like the one at Cowden (Kent) to Major-General Woodhouse who died in 1845, and another at Purton (Wilts) richly decorated with an anchor and key. On a handsome modern lyre-ended chest tomb at Beaconsfield (Bucks) the end panel is finely carved with a coat of arms supported by two figures and surmounted by two visored helmets and a ram **(58)**.

Other churchyards where coats of arms are found include Bovey Tracey (Devon), Kington St Michael (Wilts), Netherbury (Dorset) and Otley (N Yorks). The group of eight early cast-iron slabs at Burrington (Herefs) nearly all have coats of arms in relief, and in the churchyard at Upper Cam (Gloucs) is a handsome modern headstone dated 1941. On a chest tomb at Seend (Wilts) an armorial shield occupies the end panel; unfortunately it has been inserted upside down **(59)**.

59 A heraldic shield inserted upside down at Seend, Wilts

In Thomas Gray's famous *Elegy Written in a Country Churchyard* one of the lesser known verses reads:

> The boast of heraldry, the pomp of pow'r'
> And all that beauty, all that wealth e'er gave,
> Awaits like th'inevitable hour,
> The paths of glory lead but to the grave.

8 Inscriptions and epitaphs

The inscription on a churchyard memorial is more than just a record of who is buried; where they lived and when, at what age they died and who grieved for them. We also learn what were the trades and occupations of the day, even if it was only 'beloved wife and mother' and occasionally, particularly on slate, we learn who carved the stone. Epitaphs tell us something of the moral judgements of the day and as such they are mirrors of the social scene, of the tragedies of infant mortality and accidental deaths, the 'pale consumption' and other fatal diseases. The recording of churchyard memorials provides a vital insight into the history of the parish, not only for local historians but for genealogists; the thousands of people who are members of Family History Societies provide an invaluable contribution to this particular arm of local knowledge.

The lettering on a memorial is a link, a communication, via the stonemason, between the living and the dead, and as such the carver has to use his skill and intuition to provide a memorial that fills that purpose.

The art of writing, which was developed in the mediaeval monastic scriptoria such as Lindisfarne, was during the Middle Ages the prerogative of church and state. It was not until copybooks became widely available that the skills of writing spread to the population as a whole. Copybooks were engraved on copper plates for printing, the origin of what became known as copper-plate handwriting. Very few copybooks have survived; they were issued in paper wrappers for the use of learners, and were destroyed by repeated handling. The revival of calligraphy in the seventeenth and eighteenth centuries was directly related to the increase in business and commerce, and the rise of the scribe to the position of clerk or secretary. Writing masters, who kept their own writing-schools, were held in high esteem, and writing with a pen became a desirable skill for the children of the wealthy. The new styles spread rapidly into the tombstone trade, where they have survived best in the areas of slate, such as Leicestershire and the surrounding counties, the West Yorkshire district around Morley and Otley, and the West Country.

The earliest inscribed memorials date from the beginning of the seventeenth century, about the same time that carved lettering first appeared on buildings. The inscriptions on the early seventeenth-century memorials are almost without exception in the Roman alphabet which was perfected in the second century and is still in use today. The lettering is erratic, sometimes almost crude, yet strongly cut with a charm and a vigour which makes it instantly recognisable in a churchyard today. There are excellent early examples on chest tombs at Alderley (Gloucs) dated 1589, at Podimore (see p. 58) and Cucklington, both 1617 and at South Brewham (Somset) 1623. One of the earliest is the chest tomb at Standish (Gloucs) to William Beard. The inscription reads:

HERE RESTETH THE BODY OF SAMUELL BEARD YEAMAN WHO
DECEASED THE 8 DAY OF JUNE WAIGHTING FOR A JOYFULL
REZURRECTION UNTO GLORY ANNO DOMINI 1653

Another at West Knoyle (Wilts) in strong Roman lettering records that Henry White, Gent, who died in 1674

WAS MESSENGER TO 3 MOST EMINENT KINGS OF ENGLAND VIZ:
K JAMES, K CHARLES THE FIRST AND TO OUR PRESENT
SOVERAIGNE K CHARLES THE 2.

The words were often contracted, with the vertical strokes of THE combined, and spelling can show interesting variations. Words were close together with little space in between, and were sometimes split in the middle at the end of a line, or carried out into the border. Some words, notably 'ye' were inserted above the line as though put in afterwards. The churchyards of the Forest of Dean (Gloucs) have graphic examples of memorial lettering from the early seventeenth century; there is a particularly good example at Awre to Ann Whit who died in 1664 **(Plate 25)**. At Broad Hinton (Wilts) a well-preserved stone commemorating Henry Witt illustrates how the space has sometimes been misjudged **(60)**:

HERE LYETH THE BODY OF
HENRY WITT WHO DEPARTE^D
THIS LIFE APRIL Y^e 2: 1685
AS YOU ARE NOW SO ONCE
WAS I, IN HELTH AND STRENGTH
THOUGH HERE I LYE
AS I AM NOW SOE THOU SHALT
BE, PREPARE FOR DEATH DAND (sic)
FOLLOW ME

During the eighteenth century headstones, particularly slates, were often divided into three sections. At the head of the stone was either a calligraphic device such as a winged hourglass or an angel, or a highly ornate calligraphic letter; below that would be the facts relating to the deceased, and finally an epitaph. There was a dramatic increase in lettering styles, largely due to the use of printing in trade and industry and the spread of trade cards for advertising. Rapid developments in printing and typefounding meant that affordable illustrated writing manuals with a whole new range of lettering designs became available to craftsmen in all parts of the country. By the end of the century lettering had developed into the sophisticated designs that we see in churchyards today, particularly in areas of slate, which has a greater durability and where the mason's signature is more likely to have survived. The calligraphic influence from the spread of penmanship with finely cut flowing italics replaced the heavier relief work of the previous century. Intricately carved capital letters appeared, with some of the best on the ledgers of the West Yorkshire

*60 Early lettering on a
stone, 1681, at
Broad Hinton, Wilts*

churchyards of Morley and Lightcliffe, where there are also angels in the spandrels. Frequently the word in the head of the stone such as 'In' or 'Memory' was highly decorated with flowing lines and curved tendrils. The surround of the stone was often delicately tooled; there is a fine specimen to the Spence family, 1768, at St Mary Arden, Market Harborough (Leics) in a churchyard where the stones have been moved to form a fence round the ruined church. There are others at a number of Midland churchyards including Breedon-on-the-Hill, Rothley, Swithland and Syston (Leics) and Desborough (Hants) **(61)**.

Another superb example is carved on a fine-textured slate on the church wall at Lelant (Cnwll) to Captain Richard Curgenven of the Royal Navy, who died in 1784 aged 47; the slate is signed by Richard Ofman **(62)**. The mason would sign the stone with a flourish, as though proud of his achievement; often they would add the word Sculptor or Engraver, itself a title more often associated with silver or metalwork, sometimes with the location of their workshop.

Further north inscriptions on stone have survived well. At Bewcastle there are several headstones with inscriptions on both sides and a number of contrasting styles. A stone to Thomas Routledge, 1747, has a rounded script, while a neighbouring one, has strongly cut lettering in relief to another Thomas Routledge, 1729. Among the red sandstone memorials at Morland (Cumb) is a stone crudely carved in large letters commemorating John Jackson and his wife Elizabeth, who died in 1739 and 1740 respectively.

More sophisticated is the chest tomb at Beechingstoke (Wilts) commemorating William Pierce, 'Late Collector of Excise' who died in 1789. The second panel records a child aged eighteen months with a different surname. **(63)**

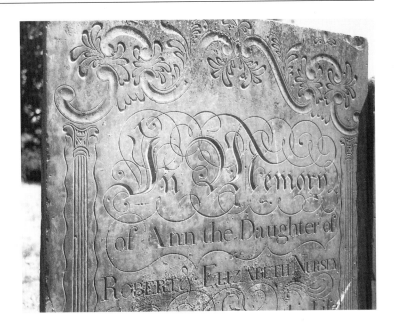

61 A finely decorated slate at Desborough, Northants

For the Cornishman making ends meet has always been difficult; the sea, the land and the mining industry were hard taskmasters before the motor car brought the era of the tourist. Here there were few grand houses or wealthy land owners requiring lavish monuments; those there were would have had their memorials inside the church. So one gets a feeling that the naive and engaging angel heads of the seventeenth century were carved by local craftsmen for ordinary working folk whose simple and hardworking lifestyle is reflected in the carving. During the early eighteenth century these were transformed into charming calligraphic angels in a wide variety of styles as the carvers began to experiment with the craft of penmanship, introducing fine lines and calligraphic flourishes. The work still has an engaging naiveté, lacking the sophistication of the early Georgian influence in other parts of the country. In an area around St Teath is a group of headstones where the opening word 'here', written in lower case, has interesting squiggles forming a banner to the upright. The angel heads have an astonishing variety of hair and wing designs; many have a wide-eyed expression as though taken by surprise. They can be found in any number of Cornish churchyards such as Cardinham, Lanivet (**64**), St Minver, St Kew and many more. Both they and the inscriptions lend themselves to the technique of rubbing, using a waxed crayon or heelball; a good way of interesting the young in our churchyard heritage.

By the early nineteenth century it was common to find several typefaces on a single panel, like the memorials to the Keene family at Minety (Wilts). In the same county the churchyard at Purton is full of examples of nineteenth-century inscriptions. A beautifully inscribed slate in the churchyard wall at St Levan (Cnwll) to Elizabeth Roberts, 1810, has a highly decorated 'In Memory' in the head of the stone and plainer lettering beneath.

As new and experimental typefaces came into circulation they were rapidly copied, superseding the calligraphic influence. They had odd names: Fat-face, Tuscan, Egyptian,

62 *(left) A finely carved and signed slate at Lelant, Cornwall*

63 *(below) Epitaph and occupation on a chest tomb, 1788, at Beechingstoke, Wilts*

*64 Cornish angel-
head and epitaph,
Lanivet, Cornwall*

Sans Serif, Grotesque, (known colloquially as Grots), and often several different typefaces were used on the same stone, producing a striking effect like the contemporary title-page. These 'modern' typefaces generally had broad vertical strokes and slender horizontal ones with fine serifs. The uprights were decorated in a variety of forms, and many of these are best illustrated on the brass plates of the Cotswolds; there are many fine examples at Painswick (Gloucs). Such delicate designs were not so easily carved on the rougher surfaces of stone, where low relief carving produced a better definition. Throughout the nineteenth century a typeface known as slab-serif, a bold geometric design either incised or in relief and often seen on early cast iron labels was the most common design on stone.[1]

The new typefaces were also particularly suited to the untextured surface of slate, and were rapidly adopted by the letter-cutters of all the slate areas. In the churchyards of St Endellion and Egloshayle (Cnwll) are several headstones with the 'modern' typefaces used to dramatic effect. One of the best is a slate to Hannah Fishley, 1850, at St Endellion with shadowed lettering **(65)**, and a 'title-page' slate to Charity Kellow, 1855. At a time when in England as a whole lettering standards were beginning to go downhill, the slate cutters of the West Country and the Midlands were still producing finely-lettered work. At Bridestowe (Devon) **(66)** and a number of surrounding churchyards are headstones with toothy skulls and strongly cut epitaphs. A group of stones in the peaceful old churchyard at Oddington (Gloucs) are mellowed with lichens and leaning in the sun. They are dated between 1860 and 1880 and are signed by Chambers of Stow; the word 'To' in the head of the stone is carved in shadow grot. A stone at Saddleworth (Yorks), with angel heads in

65 *'Modern' typeface lettering on a slate at St Endellion, Cornwall*

the spandrels, is carved with a great variety of typefaces as though the carver had got hold of a printer's catalogue and was trying them all out.

Elsewhere, as the Industrial Revolution brought improved transport and the commercialisation of quarry-cut stones and machine-cut lettering, standards began to fall. Hand-cut lettering was still carried out, but had somehow lost its sparkle. The Victorians, so preoccupied with funerals and mourning, chose foreign marbles and granite for their fulsome epitaphs while the trade mason flourished and the cemeteries expanded. Lettering styles lost their vigour, becoming plainer and heavier sans-serifs or grots, sometimes with shadow effects. Even in Cornwall horrors began to appear: at Germoe is a memorial (1853) with mass-produced lead letters set into a crude granite slab.

In our own century the Arts and Crafts movement has been a lone voice in the wilderness, striving to improve standards in all areas of design. William Morris was not himself involved in memorial design, but his own memorial at Kelmscot (Oxon) is elegantly lettered, as is the brass plate to Ernest Gimson on a ledger at Sapperton (Gloucs). In 1906 Edward Johnston published his book *Writing and Illuminating and Lettering* which became a bible on the principles of good lettering, and his pupil Eric Gill became one of the best-known sculptors of the twentieth century.

From this dedicated small band has come a growing and gifted body of modern letter-

66 Skull and crossbones, Bridestowe, Devon

The inscription on the headstone reads:

MEMENTO MORI ☙ VITA BREVIS

Here lieth the Body of William
the Son of Henry Crofsman
And Agnes his wife of this Parifh
Who was Buried the 9th day of Augu
Anno Domini 1759   Ætatis Suæ 26

Weep not dear friends it is in vain
Your lofs is my Eternal gain
For I am gone in peace to reft,
With faints and angels that are bleft

Death foon Eclipt'd my morning Sun

cutters producing innovative and inspirational work in all areas of sculpture. With compassion and sensitivity they have been able to bring their own individuality to their work without losing sight of the main object of commemoration. John Betjeman's slate at St Enodoc (Cnwll) is a prime example. The book produced by *Memorials by Artists*[2] is a superb illustration of what can be achieved, and has done much to spread the word, literally. To choose but two, there is a slate memorial in the calligraphic style to Sally Ann Coombes in the churchyard at Gunthorpe (Norfk) by David Baker; and at Fairford (Gloucs) is a headstone in Portland stone by Rory Young to Michael Peachey, who died at the age of eighteen. The inscription reads:

> Remember his youth, humour and idealism.
> Pray here with him for peace and freedom in your home
> and throughout the world.

Epitaphs

The study of inscriptions and epitaphs provides us with a fascinating and entertaining insight into the lives of the ordinary people who lived and worked in that parish. They provide a contemporary record of how they died and who mourned for them; at a time of high mortality and killer diseases they reflect the attitudes to death and offer us an exceptional insight into local history. Few could fail to be amused by Sarah Jarvis of Corsham who died in 1753 at the age of 107. Her inscription records that 'she had Fresh Teeth shortly before she died.'

Weever, writing in 1631[3] suggested that epitaphs should consist of 'the name, the age, the deserts, the dignities, the state, the praises both of body and mind, the good or bad fortunes in the life, and the manner and time of the death of the person therein interred,' advice which does not seem to have been taken until the eulogistic epitaphs of the early nineteenth century.

Inscriptions on early memorials were generally brief, partly because the surface area of the stones was small, but also because the lettering skills of the time were limited. An exception to this is the very early brass slate at Duntisbourne Rous (Gloucs), a remarkable survival; it was not uncommon at that time to give the the names of dead chidren to subsequent ones.

> An elegie of Elizabeth Jefferis Wydowe of John Jefferis of Dunsburne upon his
> death who deceased the XII day of September 1611.
> Two bodies in one united hart conteind
> Fast linct in loyall league of true affection
> But Death that such a sweet content disdain'd
> Mad of one half to immanure discretion
> One half yet lives alasse why lives it longer
> It lives to make my greife and sorrowes stronger
> Yet till the time my fatall thred be spannd
> My halfe shall pay perpetuall obsequies
> As fresh as when my firme love first begunne
> And deck thy hearse with endless elegies
> When in self same hearse desired shrine
> My body shall the last rest take by thine.

> We had VIII children
> IIII sonnes and IIII daughters as followeth
> John   Elizabeth
> George   Ann
> Thomas   Susana
> John   Elizabeth

Towards the end of the seventeenth century epitaphs were short, with a distinctly moral tone. One of the commonest, still found in nearly every churchyard reads:

> As you are now so once was I;
> As I am now so you shall be;
> Therefore prepare to follow me.

A more graphic variation of this is on the wall of the ruined charnel-house in the churchyard of Bury St Edmunds (Suffk). It commemorates Sarah Worton, who died in 1698:

> Good people all, as you
> Pass by, looke round
> See how Corpes do lye
> For as you are, some time were we
> And as we are so you must be.

The moral tone is also reflected on a chest tomb at Lanteglos-by-Camelford (Cnwll) to Mary Hodge who died in 1684, followed by her son in 1699:

> Heare lyes the mother and her hopeful son
> Their days are past, their race is run
> May you behold as well think on
> Your days doe pass and will be gone
> The grave must be your lodging place
> Be carefull then to Run your Race
> Running so well you may obtain
> Your dying then will be your Gaine.

During the eighteenth century epitaphs became longer and more varied, providing a fascinating insight into local trades and professions, causes of death and family relationships. Child mortality is recorded time and again: on a headstone at Lydney (Gloucs) commemorating Mary Parry who died in 1758 at the age of three. The short verse reads:

> Her time was short and longer was her rest
> God call'd her hence because he saw it best.

On a headstone at St Endellion (Cnwll) is the unusual inscription to 'four Children who all Expir'd in Embrio's' **(67)**.

In the days when there was no effective relief for pain and illness, epitaphs like these can be found in nearly every churchyard:

> Affliction sore long time I bore
> All human help was vain
> Till God did please Death should me seize
> And ease me of my pain.

Also, remembering diseases which have since been almost eradicated:

> The pale consumption struck the fatal blow
> The stroke was harsh but the effect came slow

113

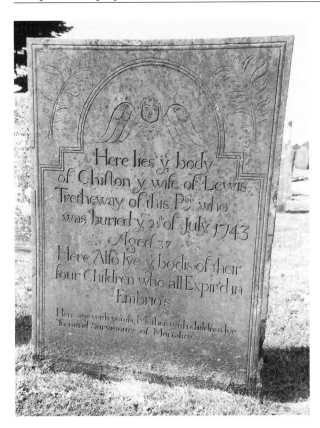

> With wasting pains Christ saw me sore oppress'd
> Pity'd my soul and kindly gave me rest.

Trades and professions are well represented and lend themselves to allegorical interpretation. The following epitaph to a blacksmith is found in several churchyards; this one is at Thursley (Surrey):

> My sledge and hammer lie reclined
> My bellows too have lost their wind
> My fire's extinct, my forge decay'd
> And in the dust my vice is laid
> My coal is spent, my iron's gone
> My nails are drove, my work is done
> My fire-dried corpse lies here at rest
> And smoke-like soars up to be bless'd.

There are several similar ones, including those at Upleadon (Gloucs) and Shotley (Nthumb). Clockmakers also lend themselves to allegory. The following one in prose is at Lydford, (Devon):

Here lies, in horizontal position the outside case of George Routleigh, Watchmaker, whose abilites in that line were an honour to his profession, Integrity was the Mainspring and Prudence the Regulator of all the actions of his life. Humane, generous and liberal, his hands never stopped till he had relieved distress. So nicely regulated were all his motions that he never went wrong, except when set a-going by people who did not know his Key; even then he was easily set right again. He had the Art of disposing his time so well that his hours glided away in one continual round of pleasure and delight, Until an unlucky minute put a period to his existence. He departed this life November 14, 1802, aged 57, wound up, in hopes of being taken in hand by his Maker. And of being thoroughly cleaned, repaired and set a-going in the world to come.

The message, more concisely put, is the well-known epitaph to Thomas Pierce, clockmaker of Berkeley (Gloucs).

Here lieth Thomas Pierce whom no man taught
Yet he in iron, brass and silver wrought
He jacks and clocks and watches with art made
And mended too when others work did fade
Of Berkeley five times Mayor this artist was
And yet this mayor, this artist was but grass
When his own watch was down on the last day
He that made watches had not made a key
To wind it up, but useless it must lie
Until he rise again no more to die.

In the same churchyard is the so-called 'Jester's tomb' to Dicky Pearce, who was Court Jester at Berkeley Castle and was killed when he fell from the musicians' gallery in 1725.

Here lies the Earl of Suffolk's fool
Men call'd him Dicky Pearce
His folly serv'd to make folks laugh
When wit and mirth were scarce.
Poor Dick Alas! Is dead and gone
What signifies to cry?
Dickys enough are left behind
To laugh at by and by.

Ralph Bigland[4] says that this epitaph was written by Dean Swift, Chaplain to Charles, Earl of Berkeley, whose own epitaph was also written by Swift.

In the churchyard at Bromsgrove (Worcs) is a pair of large headstones to two engineers, Thomas Scaife and Joseph Rutherford. The stones are painted black with white lettering, and in the head of each is a low relief carving of a locomotive of the period, picked out in black paint against a white background. They died in an accident caused by 'the Explosion of an Engine Boiler on Tuesday the 10 of November 1840'; they were 26 and 32 respectively. The epitaph on the Scaife stone reads:

> My engine now is cold and still
> No water does my boiler fill
> My coke affords its flame no more
> My days of usefulness are o'er
> My wheels deny their noted speed
> No more my guiding hands they heed
> My whistle too has lost its tone
> Its shrill and thrilling sounds are gone
> My valves are now thrown open wide
> My flanges all refuse to guide
> My clacks, also, though once so strong
> Refuse to aid the busy throng
> No more I feel each urging breath
> My steam is now condensed in death
> Life's railway's o'er, each station's past
> In death I'm stopped and rest at last
> Farewell dear friends and cease to weep
> In Christ I'm safe, in Him I sleep.

Accidental death

Accidental death is common, and is often described in some detail. At Lansallos (Cnwll), with an identical one at Talland is a slate to a smuggler, John Perry, Mariner,

> 'who was unfortunately kill'd by a Cannon Ball by a person unknown in ye year 1779 aged 24 years, June ye 5th.'
> In prime of life my suddenly
> Sad tidings to relate
> Here view my utter destiny
> And pity my sad fate.
> I by a shot which rapid flew
> Was instantly struck dead
> Lord pardon the offender who
> My precious blood did shed
> Grant him to rest and forgive me
> All I have done amiss
> And that I may rewarded be
> With everlasting bliss.

*68 Accidental death,
Morwenstow,
Cornwall*

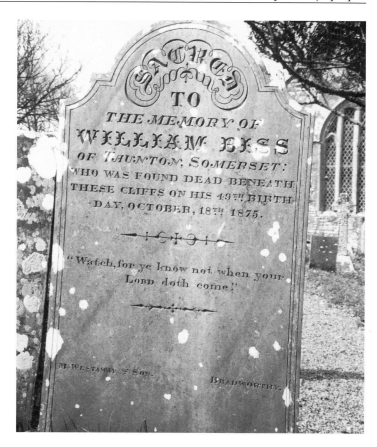

At Littledean (Gloucs) is a memorial describing in graphic detail a mining disaster which obviously devasted a small community. The youngest to die was James Meredith, aged 12.

> These four youths were suddenly called into Eternity on Tuesday the 6th day of April 1819 by an awful dispensation of the Almighty. The link of a chain employed to lower them into Bilston Pit breaking they were precipitated to the bottom of the Pit. Their bones literally dashed to pieces their bodies thus presenting a frightful and appalling spectacal (sic) to all who beheld them. They were interred in one grave on the Friday following being Good Friday April 9 1819. A funeral sermon was preached on the mournful occasion on Sunday April 25 1819 in the Church of Little Deane before a congregation of 2500 people on the following text which it was judged advisable to record upon their Tomb as a suitable admonition for the benefit of all survivors.
>
> Luke XIII vs 1,2 & 3.
> Swift flew the appointed messenger of death
> And in a moment stopt their mortal breath.
> Art thou prepared as suddenly to die?
> 'Tis mercy's call O list unto the cry.

It is interesting to note that inscriptions during the seventeenth and eighteenth centuries contain very few biblical texts or other statements of faith. It wasn't until the early nineteenth century that the message of salvation began to appear, often in verbose and eulogistic epitaphs. This is carried to excess in the epitaph at Wylyle (Wilts) which is thought to have been written by Thomas Dampier, rector there for 72 years, from 1759 to 1831.

> The Great, Vain Polish'd Marbles raise
> the those who seldom merit Praise
> But here the Widow and the Friend
> A man of real Worth commend
> The Neighbour whose Calm, Peaceful Life
> Gave no Disturbance, made no Strife
> The Husband, the Relation Dear
> The Christian Pious and Sincere
> A Character so Far and True
> None but the Virtuous will pursue
> Who when the last Dread Trumpets Sound
> Shall Rise and be with Glory Crowned.

In the days before the arrival of the railways gave families access to the seaside, death by drowning was common. At Dymock (Gloucs), where a mediaeval road runs through the churchyard, is an epitaph on a chest tomb to the two Hooper boys who drowned in the River Leadon in 1824 at the ages of 28 and 18.

> In perfect health we went from home
> Not thinking that our Glass was run.
> The running flood of water strong
> It did our Bodies overcome
> For God above who thought it fit
> To lay our body in the Deep
> Now parents dear forbear to mourn
> We wait the Resurrection morn.

A headstone at Hanbury (Worcs) has a graphic carving of Henry Parry falling under the wheels of his horse and cart in 1847 **(69)**:

> Our life hangs by a single thread
> It soon is cut and we are dead
> Then boast not reader of thy might
> Alive at noon and dead at night.
> Like a flower I was cut down
> And left my parents dear to mourn
> Ah! Twenty one years was but young
> They soon pass'd by and I was gone.

69 Henry Parry is trampled by his horse, 1847, Hanbury, Worcs

The morning sun on me arose
At night I took my last repose
Let my quick fate a warning be
To all that come my grave to see.

With the improvements in transport in the middle of the eighteenth century some people were obliged to find work in towns and cities. An epitaph at Miserden (Gloucs) reads:

In memory of William Ferne of this Parish (Plasterer) whose death was occasioned by a fall from a Building in London July 14th 1861 in the 44th year of his age, leaving a widow and six children.

Another sad loss of life was the accident that happened to Ann Collins, a barmaid of Kings Stanley (Gloucs) who died in 1804 aged 49:

'Twas as she tript from cask to cask
In at a bung hole quickly fell
Suffocation was her task
She had not time to say farewell.

Another woman who came to an untimely end was Hannah Twynnoy, who in 1703 was killed by a tiger that had escaped from a travelling circus. Her famous headstone is at Malmesbury (Wilts).

> In bloom of Life
> She's snatch'd from hence
> She had not room
> To make defence
> For Tyger fierce
> Took Life away
> And here she lies
> In a bed of clay
> Until the Resurrection Day.

Murders

Murders are also not forgotten. On an odd-shaped stone at Egloshayle (Cnwll) is recorded a brutal crime:

> To Nevell Norway, merchant of Wadebridge aged 39 who was murdered on the 8th February 1840.
> He left behind him a widow and six children unprovided for. A subscription of £3,500 was made for their use, a noble testimony of the generous feeling of the public and the high estimation in which his amiable and spotless character was held.

On a stone at Littledean (Gloucs) is a inscription which reads:

> Sacred to the memory of Samule Beard, late a Police Sergeant at Littledean who was brutally beaten by four men at the Speech House when in the discharge of his duty on the night of the 17 August and died from the effects on 24 August 1761 aged 37 years.
> Esteemed and respected by the whole Force for his Integrity, Punctuality and Exemplary discharge of his duties.

It is not surprising in a maritime nation to find epitaphs recording disasters at sea. This one from Padstow (Cnwll) is found in several places:

> Here lyes the body of Thomas Pearse of this towne, Mariner, who was buried the fourth day of June Anno Domini 1709 aged 54 years.
> Tho' Boysterous winds and Billows sore
> Have toss'd me To and Fro
> By God's decree in Spight of both
> I rest me here below
> When at an Anchor now I lye

With many of our Fleet
One day I shall set Sayl agaain
Our Saviour for to meet.

Also at Padstow is the sad tale of Thomas and Mary Deacon, who lost a son aged five, then another aged three and a third who drowned at the age of nineteen. Finally their daughter Alberta died on April 28th 1863 aged thirteen months. Her epitaph is appealing:

Dear prattling child to all our hearts most dear
Long shall we bathe thy memory with a tear
Farewell to promising on earth to dwell
Sweetest of fondlings, best of babes farewell.

Occupations
Occupations are a rich source of local history; on the outside north wall of the church at Stroud (Gloucs) is a whole row of brass plates which have evidently been removed from memorials. They make up an fascinating picture of the tradespeople of Stroud in the early eighteenth century: there are clothiers, of course, together with the expected butcher and baker, but there is also a blacksmith, a surgeon, a mason, a confectioner, a maltster and, more interestingly, a peruke-maker and a stay-maker. In the same churchyard on the ground is a large plate commemorating Richard Merrett 'watch and clockmaker, who died under inoculation December 17, 1767 aged 57 years'.

He was an ingenious mechanic, sincere friend and Christian true to the faith
of his Redeemer. It was his request therefore let no sacrilegious hand disturb
his ashes but permit them to rest in this gloomy mansion till the last trumpet
shall awaken him to Life and Immortality.
Let those who to these awful Cells repair
To waste an hour or ease the soul of care
Stop one short moment near his plaintive stone
And with the tears of friendship mix their own.
Then take the last advice by Merrett given
Be virtuous now, leave all the rest to heaven.

There is another memorial which mentions inoculation at Mere (Wilts).
    An ambiguous inscription at Chipping Norton (Oxon) records the death in 1763 of:

Phillis wife of John Humphreys, Ratcatcher, who has lodged in many town
and travelled far and near. By Age and Death shee (sic) is struck down to her
last lodging here.

Trades are often represented by tools of the trade carved on the stone, like the barber's tools on William Haslam's headstone (1786) at Broadway (Worcs) (see p.101) and the thatchers tools on a stone at Long Sutton (Lincs). In Gloucestershire at Frampton-on-

Severn is the headstone to William Keyes (1795) who was a blacksmith, although his memorial is carved with musical instruments.

The oldest memorial to a soldier is said to be the one at Kingscote (Gloucs) (see p.66) which is dated 1656. The inscription is still legible almost 350 years later.

> HERE LYETH THE BODY OF TROYLUS KINGSCOTE GENT WHO
> DID SERVICE AS A COMMANDER FOR THE PRINCE OF ORANGE
> 40 YEARES AND BEING 80 YEARES OLD ENDED THIS LIFE THE
> 10TH DAY OF SEPTEMBER ANNO DOMINI 1656.

Better known is the headstone to a soldier buried at Winchester (Hants):

> In Memory of Thomas Thetcher, a Grenadier in the North Regiment of
> Hampshire Militia 'who died of a Violent Fever contracted by drinking Small
> Beer when hot, 12 May 1674.'
>
> In grateful remembrance of whose universal goodwill towards his comrades
> this stone was placed here at their expence (sic) as a small testimony of their
> regard and concern.
> Here sleeps in peace a Hampshire Grenadier
> Who caught his death by drinking cold small beer
> Soldiers be wise from his untimely fall
> When ye're hot drink Strong or none at all.

Other occupations are less predictable. On a worn stone at Cheltenham (St Mary's) is the odd epitaph to John Higgs, which is now largely defaced. He died in 1825:

> Here lies John Higgs
> A famous man for killing pigs
> For killing pigs was his delight
> Both morning, afternoon and night.
> Both heats and colds he did endure
> Which no physician e'er could cure
> His knife is laid, his work is done
> I hope to Heaven his soul is gone.

In the same churchyard the following well-known epitaph has disappeared:

> Here lies I with my two daughters
> We died from drinking Cheltenham waters
> If we had stuck to Epsom Salts
> We wouldn't be lying in these here vaults

Servants are well represented: a ledger outside the churchdoor at Stockton (Wilts) is a memorial to Anne Raxworthy, lady's maid, who died in 1829.

> She was a worthy and faithful servant for nearly fifty years and a good Christian. She was buried below at her own request.

It was uncommon to find women's occupations noted on their memorials, but at Bellingham (Nthumb) is a headstone recording a midwife. There is an unusual dedication to two women at Saltash (Cnwll):

> This stone is erected by the noncommissioned officers and men of the Plymouth division of the Royal Marines in memory of Mary May who died the 2nd October 1860 aged 76 years. Also of her mother Mary Blake who died the 7th June 1841 aged 40 years. The mother and daughter supplied the Royal Marine barracks at Stonehouse with shellfish for more than half a century and gained the good opinion of all their customers by their sterling honesty and kind and unassuming demeanour.

Set into the churchyard wall at Paul (Cnwll) is the monument to Dorothy Pentreath which was set up by Prince Loucien Bonaparte. On the stone is the fifth commandment and the claim that she was the last person to speak the Cornish language. She was said to be 102 when she died in 1777, and part of the inscription is written in Cornish.

In the churchyard at Henbury, Bristol is the well-known memorial to a slave, Scipio Africanus, 'Negro Servant of the Rt Honourable Charles William, Earl of Suffolk and Bradon, who died ye 21 December 1720 aged 18.' He was said to be a 'running footman' and his death was said to have been caused by running from London. The memorial consists of a headstone and footstone of similar size, with gold-lettered slate inserts and negro heads set into the stone. The epitaph suggests that he was conscious of his colour:

> I who was born a pagan and a slave
> Now sweetly sleep a Christian in my Grave
> What though my hue was dark my Saviors (sic) sight
> Shall change this darkness into radiant light.
> Such grace to me my lord on earth has given
> To recommend me to my Lord in heaven
> Whose glorious second coming here I wait
> With saints and angels Him to celebrate.

Enigmatic epitaphs
These are rare and are fun to seek out. This one is at English Bicknor (Gloucs) and commemorates William Cooper:

> I grive to think that I can grive (sic) no more
> For thou my loving friend.

A short epitaph to John Taylor at Chilton Foliat (Wilts) who died in 1832 expresses no regrets:

> Farewell to all beneath the sun
> I bid the world adieu
> I never found no solid mirth
> Nor happiness in you.

The brass plates of the Cotswolds are well preserved and make interesting reading. This one at Sapperton is a sad reflection on family life to Mary daughter of William and Jane Gardner who died 31st May 1792 aged 44:

> Her husband devoid of humanity to perpetuate her memory, her SON in respectful remembrance caus'd this TABLET to be erected over her sleeping dust.

Another at Duntisbourne Abbotts carries a salutary message which could still apply in our own time. William Beames died in 1799 at the age of 22.

> A warning peice (sic) to all young men
> Who in their blooming age
> Misspend their time and know not when
> They must go off the stage.

St Ives (Cnwll) has a rare anagram epitaph:

> Neere to this bed sixe Sises late were laid
> Foure hopefull sons, a grandsire and a maid
> All striving which should end his journey first
> All for the well-spring of true Life did thirst
> The virgrin's elegy outweepes the rest
> Such lovely grase was stampt on face and brest.

The maid died in 1642; the anagram reads:
> Alice Sise: ills cease.

Also in Cornwall there is rumoured to be an acrostic in the churchyard at Gunwalloe, although no-one seems able to find it. It is similar to one on a brass of 1708 to Hannibal Basset in the church at Mawgan-in-Meneage:

Shall	we	all	die?
Weee	shall	die	all.
All	die	shall	wee?
Die	all	weee	shall.

It is not uncommon to find charitable bequests inscribed on early chest tombs. By the south porch at Bremhill (Wilts) is a group of early eighteenth century chest tombs commemorating the Spackman and Broome families. One records Ralph Broome of Nuthills and is carved with trumpetting cherubs. It has an inscription on the south side which reads:

> Witness his last legacy of £460 to endow a school for ye education of 60 poor children to be instructed in ye principles of the Christian Religion According to ye Church of England. His Charity to ye Poor Extended to the last by Giveing £20 to ye Poor of Lyneham where he liv'd and died.
> And £20 more to the Poor of the Parish.

On the north side is an equally fulsome epitaph:

> Beneath this stone the mortal part doth lie
> Of him who did all nations base defile
> Just and upright he was to every man
> And never failed to lend a helping hand
> Unto the poor from round about's abode
> He fed the hungry and the naked clothed
> For such good deeds our Blessed Lord doth say
> That he the giver will most surely pay.

Bremhill was the home of the parson-poet William Lisa Bowles, who was rector from 1805-1845. He had little books of epitaphs printed and circulated among his parishioners.

Another early bequest can be seen on the Prankerd memorial at Milborne Port (Somset). In strong Roman lettering it starts:

> HERE LYETH Y BODIE OF THOMAS PRANKERD BACHELOR;
> INTERRED Y 3 OF JANVARIE 1609 WHICH GAVE BY HIS WILL TO
> THE POORE OF M P 40 POUNDS TO BE AND TO REMAINE TO
> THEM FOR EVER ...

There are eighteenth-century bequests on the beautiful Adye tomb (1731) at Easton Grey and another at Burbage (Wilts); later ones can be found on the handsome Hyde memorial at Beaconsfield (Bucks), and at St Margaret's Leicester.

The last word must go to the nineteenth-century lines that are found in a number of churchyards. This one is at Burford (Oxon) and is dated 1849:

> Praises on stones are titles vainly spent
> A man's good name is his best monument.

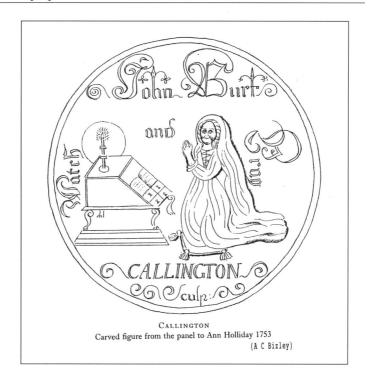

CALLINGTON
Carved figure from the panel to Ann Holliday 1753
(A C Bizley)

Slate to Ann Holliday at Callington, Cornwall. (A C Bizley)

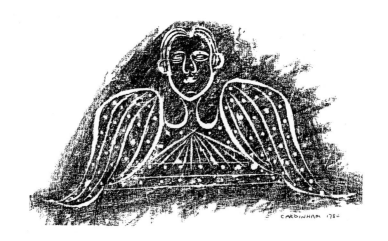

9 Materials

Before the arrival of the canals at the beginning of the nineteenth century and later the railways, the only building materials available to the village craftsman were those which could be found locally. The stone for the church, the houses, barns, walls and even for the roads would all have come from the same quarry, giving the village a feeling of harmony, as though the buildings were growing out of the land, which in a sense they were. A good example of this is the churchyard at Bibury (Gloucs) where the stone for the church, the boundary walls, the surrounding buildings and the memorials have all mellowed together into a silvery grey. In addition the stones and the cherubs carved on them have a family likeness, as though they are the work of one man.

The different qualities of each stone affect the way in which the stonemason approaches his task: the deep carving of Cotswold limestone; the finely incised lettering on slate; the relief work of Forest sandstone, the solidity of granite. The choice of stone will be one of the earliest decisions and will have a direct effect on the character of the finished memorial. We only have to look at recent modern work to appreciate the differences in character and lettering between memorials of slate and limestone. These characteristics have produced regional variations not only in building design but also in churchyard memorials. The subtle characteristics of each stone are only learnt by experience: how durable they are; where they are to be sited and how they weather; how best they respond to the chisel and the saw. This is the expertise that has been passed down from one generation of stonemasons to the next, and from master carver to student. Stone from the same quarry, even from the same bed, can have different properties, and to this day a stonemason will go in person to select the right piece of stone from the quarry.

In modern times these differences are less noticeable; it is now possible to have the stone of your choice regardless of where you live, and the insurgence of imported stones has brought a monotonous similarity to most of our churchyards and cemeteries.

Interior funerary monuments achieved a great importance in the Middle Ages, largely due to the growth of church patronage and chantry chapels. This 'luxury' trade on memorials was carried out by highly skilled carvers working in the two native 'marbles': Purbeck, which is in fact a hard limestone, in the thirteenth century and alabaster, which is a sulphate of lime and is too soft for outdoor work, during the later Middle Ages. By contrast when vernacular work began to appear in churchyards the carvers would have been what today we would call jobbing builders working on farms and barns in the locality. Possibly the local schoolmaster, as the person most likely to have the necessary lettering skills, would also have been involved.

With the revival of monumental carving after the Reformation stonemasons were amongst the most highly regarded and best paid workers. The numbers of grand houses under construction meant that there was plenty of work for skilled craftsmen and designers, and the growth of the wool trade ensured that the new and wealthy middle classes could afford lavish memorials.

The stones

Limestone

Limestone, a sedimentary rock, is made up of the tiny, often microscopic shells of sea or freshwater animals, or ooliths, compressed in layers on the sea floor over millions of years. It is rich in minute fossils and feels rough to the touch. The great limestone belt stretches from Portland to Yorkshire and the stone varies considerably in colour and texture; it is no accident that much of the best churchyard work is within this belt. Different varieties are named after the quarry from which they come: Bath, Hornton, Hopton Wood, Portland, Taynton, Thornbeck. They vary in colour from off-white to a rich honey-coloured gold. They mellow with weathering, collecting mosses and lichens, so producing the archetypal image of the English country churchyard. At one time almost every town and village would have had a quarry, and it wasn't until the early 1960s that most of the Cotswold quarries had closed.

The variations in colour and texture add character to each region: Portland stone has a close, even texture which is almost pure white; the quarry is still very much in business, as anyone visiting the church of St George Reforne will testify. In Somerset the golden brown of Ham Hill stone has been used for memorials at Brympton d'Evercy, Kilve and Milborne Port. In Wiltshire the pleasing harmony of Chilmark village is an advertisement for the fine-grained, creamy white local stone which was so conveniently near for the building of Salisbury Cathedral. Further north the Cotswolds vary from a pale cream yellow in the Bath area to the deep golden colour of the Taynton quarries north of Burford. It was from the quarries of Taynton and Burford that stone was taken to London for the rebuilding of St Paul's Cathedral after the Great Fire, where local masons from the Strong and Kempster families worked with Wren.

Because limestone is stratified, the thickness and quality of different strata can vary. For the purposes of tombstone construction two sorts are needed: weatherstone, which is a hard, coarse-grained stone suitable for the base and ledger of a chest tomb, and freestone, a finer-textured stone suitable for fine carving and able to be cut in any direction. This would have been used for the side panels of chest tombs and for headstones.

The structure of the limestone is such that while it is still in the quarry the stone retains a certain amount of natural moisture, which once the stone is quarried will migrate to the surface and cause the stone to crystallise and harden. However while the stone is still 'green' it is soft enough to be deep-carved, as is admirably demonstrated by the gadrooned corner balusters on the eighteenth-century Hanman tomb at Elmore and the Andrews chest tomb (1738) at Standish (Gloucs).

In Somerset and the neighbouring areas of Dorset the liassic limestone from Hamdon Hill, known as Ham Hill stone, has been used extensively for building, including churches and churchyard memorials. Its deep gold warms in the sun, and is seen at its best in the mellow setting of Brympton d'Evercy and in the peaceful surroundings of Stoke-sub-Hamdon. Here, two seventeenth- and early eighteenth-century chest tombs of unusual and ornate design are in danger of sinking.

By contrast the carboniferous limestone of the north of England has a colour and solidity which seems entirely appropriate to the rugged nature of the Yorkshire Dales. In the churchyard at Whittingham (Nthumb) the memorials have an engaging lack of sophistication; some have large cherub heads in half relief occupying most of the face of the stone.

The problem with limestone is that it weathers badly; while on sculpture this can have the mellowing effect of softening the contours, on inscriptions it can be disastrous. Where early inscriptions have survived, they may have been sheltered from the elements by the overhang of the ledger on a chest tomb, or by overhanging vegetation. There is a pretty rococo headstone at Northleach (Gloucs) to Will Morse who died in 1775 aged 31, with the beautiful lettering of the period still in mint condition.

The problem of weathering was overcome by fixing 'brass' plates - which are actually made of an alloy of copper and tin called latten — to the surface, and these have become an art form all of their own. They occur in places all over the limestone belt, for instance at Morland (Cumb), but the vast majority are in the Cotswolds. In a churchyard such as Painswick they reached the peak of decorative art in the Georgian period and are frequently signed by the same carvers that were responsible for much of the stone work. They vary from factual statements concerning the deceased to varied and amusing epitaphs. On a ledger at Uley (Gloucs) is a decorated plate to Roger Rutter, alias Rudder, 'who was buried August 30th 1771 having never eaten flesh, fish nor fowl during the course of his long life of 84 years.' In the neighbouring churchyard of Coaley is a plate commemorating an organist, Mary Smith, who died in 1746 aged 46. The plate shows a church organ complete with pipes, with underneath it the annotated music from Handel's *Messiah* and the words from the Book of Job, 'I know that my Redeemer liveth.'

Sandstone

Found largely in the West and North, sandstone is also sedimentary and is built up in layers. It is made up of thousands of grains of sand compressed together and cemented with minerals. It ranges in colour from a dull cream to red or blue/grey and can vary in hardness and texture. Sometimes the dividing line between limestone and sandstone is not entirely clear; some limestones can have a high proportion of sand, and some sandstones can contain a lot of chalk. The best collection of sandstone memorials is in the Forest of Dean (Gloucs), where the hard Forest stone has weathered well and a great deal of early rustic work is still in good condition. Further north the thirteenth-century memorials at Astbury (Ches) are in yellow sandstone, as are the memorials at Felling (T and W) which unfortunately are badly polluted. On two early seventeenth century chest tombs at Stringston (Somset) sandstone has been used in conjunction with blue lias, a limestone from Somerset and West Dorset. One inscription in fine lettering begins:

> With sobbinge feares I doe lament
> My woeful yeares and time ill spent ...

Red sandstone is not often seen in the churchyard; at Corsham (Wilts) is a memorial to the Brakspears, father and son who were well known Wiltshire architects at the end of the nineteenth century. At Isel (Cumb) an elaborately carved late fifteenth-century chest tomb was once inside the church. An odd memorial in red sandstone at Sherington (Bucks) has inserted limestone inscription plaques. Three carry biblical texts; the fourth has the enigmatic message:

> Reader! The name, profession and age of him whose body lies within are of little importance.

At St Mary's, Lambeth (London) which is now the Museum of Garden History, the former churchyard is now a small garden dedicated to the botanical specimens brought back to this country by the Tradescant family. The tomb of John Tradescant and his family is possibly the most elaborately decorated sandstone memorial in the country; built in 1662, it is carved on all sides in high relief with mythical beasts, flora and fauna and classical ruins.

Slate

This is formed from mud which has been heated to high temperatures underground. At one time there were extensive slate quarries in the Midlands, but now it is quarried only in Wales, Cornwall and Cumbria. It is smooth and hard and splits easily, which is why it is suitable for roofing slates. Its close, impervious texture makes it suitable for fine, incised lettering and low relief sculpture. For many years Cornish slate came from the Delabole quarry near Camelford, but they are no longer able to provide slate of a suitable quality and carvers are now having to go to North Wales for their supplies.

In Cornwall there is a whole group of panelled slate chest tombs at Mawgan-in-Pydar and at Warbstow is a long row of raised ledgers dating from 1735-1826.

One of the finest regional groups of slates came from the quarries at Swithland (Leics). They can be seen in any of the surrounding churchyards and their survival is a testimony to the durability of the material.

The most handsome memorial in slate is the large sarcophagus to Sir John and Lady Danvers at Swithland, dated 1745. It is built with one third of the tomb outside the churchyard wall in order that Sir John's dog could be buried with him. In fine slate, it has brass plates with inscriptions on three sides: 'When young I sayl'd to India, east and west, but aged in this port must lye at rest.' Beneath is a ship and a church on a hill. And on the south side: 'Be chearfull (sic) O man and labour to live, the mercifull God a blessing will give' with scenes of ploughing and building. The slate panels are carved with heraldic crests and the tomb is surrounded by wrought iron railings with spearhead finials and urns on the corners.

One of the great bonuses of slate is that signatures have often survived. On the beautiful slate to Ann Holliday (1753) on the outside of the porch at Callington (Cnwll) are two trumpetting angels in low relief holding back drapes, while a smaller angel holding a cross and banner tramples triumphantly on the skeleton of death. The inscription is flanked by classical pillars, and at the bottom inside a circle is the figure of a woman kneeling at a *prie-dieu*. The slate is signed by John Burt, Sculp. (see p.126)

70 Tomb cut from solid block of granite, Bovey Tracey, Devon

Granite

This is a hard volcanic rock which solidifies under pressure deep in the earth. It is made up of hard crystalline minerals which may be white, black, grey or pink. It can be rough-cut or polished and its durability is much favoured by monumental masons. Granite grave slabs of mediaeval origin can be found in a number of churchyards in the West Country, but two memorials at Bovey Tracey (Devon) are good examples of its durability. One is a chest tomb which, excluding the ledger, is cut from a single piece of granite. It has primitive carvings of angels with outspread wings on one side and on the other two mythical beasts, possibly a lion and a unicorn, in low relief. The date is 1678 **(70)**. The second memorial has three small obelisks on the gable, carved with a mermaid, a flower and a thistle; the east end had a coat of arms with a thistle above. On the front is a long inscription and the date, 1655. These memorials are unique in their design and also because it is rare to find fine carving in granite. There is another good example in the Manning tomb at Morwenstow (Cnwll).

In the second half of the nineteenth century the ubiquitous Celtic cross, together with granite curbs and coloured chippings reappeared in churchyards all over the country. At Padstow (Cnwll) are two large and ugly granite monoliths with slate inserts; they are completely out of place.

Artificial stones

These are rarely found among churchyard memorials, the exception being Coade stone, which was invented by the Coade family and manufactured in London from 1769 to about 1840. It is not in fact stone, but is made from fired clay similar to terracotta, and was used extensively for architectural decoration. Its most successful use as a memorial is in the monument to Warren Hastings at Daylesford (Gloucs), an elegant urn on a Greek-Revival podium, still in pristine condition today. The inscription reads simply, Warren Hastings, 1818.

Sharing pride of place with the Tradescant tomb at St Mary's, Lambeth are two memorials in Coade stone; one is a tall sarcophagus in Greek Revival style to Admiral Bligh who achieved fame as Captain Bligh of the Bounty and brought the breadfruit tree from the Marquesas to the West Indies. The second is a square sarcophagus also with antefixae and with a serpent entwined round a classical urn. It commemorates William Sealy who was a colleague of Coade in the making of artificial stone.

In the churchyard at Woodbridge (Suffk) is a memorial to James Pulham (1765-1830) who with his brother Obadiah invented an artificial stone called Pulhamite, said by Burgess to be 'practically indistinguishable from Portland stone'[1] and found on plaques in Doric Place, Woodbridge and on a headstone at nearby Wrentham.

Brick

Chest tombs made of brick are relatively rare. They can be found in a few churchyards in Suffolk, including Burgh which has a coffin-shaped brick tomb with a stone ledger. Along the Avon valley north of Salisbury (Wilts) there are several groups of red brick chest tombs in churchyards such as Great Durnford.

At Stoke Poges (Bucks) the poet Thomas Gray, who died in 1771, lies buried under a modest brick chest tomb where his mother and aunt were also interred. The tall monument in the adjoining field was erected by his admirers in 1799 'among the scenes celebrated by the great lyric and elegiac poet'. Gray's Elegy continues to be the best known churchyard poem. Under a yew tree in the same churchyard is a collection of bodystones, including a brick one. Behind the church a line of modern graves commemorates four boys who died in an accident at Lands End in 1985. One of the headstones is carved with a football.

Marble

Before it became the general material of choice for memorials, marble was used for some of the grandest early churchyard monuments. The Waller memorial (1687) at Beaconsfield (Bucks) is a tall marble obelisk on a chest tomb with stone drapery and is quite unique for such an early date.

In the churchyard at East Hagbourne (Oxon) is the splendid chest tomb in white marble and stone to Thomas Phillips 'whose known skill and diligence in his profession, joined with great probity in his dealings gave him that reputation in business which recommended him to be carpenter to their Majesties King George the First and King George the Second. He died the 14th day of August 1736 aged 47 years.'

Marble is often used for inserted plaques; the Seymour memorial (1825) at Seend (Wilts) has marble plaques on all sides and a marble urn, and there are others at Box (Wilts). Slate is also used for insertions, well demonstrated on the group of seventeenth-century chest tombs at Kilmersdon (Somset) where slate has been used very effectively, and the inscriptions are still totally legible (see p.60).

71 *Cast iron pedestal at Madeley Shropshire*

Other materials

These include include *wood*, which has been used for centuries, particularly in the areas where stone was not available, but does not last. Some have survived occasionally in the form of graveboards; crosses are still used as grave markers until such time as a stone can be erected. A wooden memorial shaped to depict the stern of a boat at Mawgan-in-Pydar (Cnwll) was erected in memory of ten men who drifted ashore on December 15th 1846 and were found frozen to death in the morning. One of them, Jemmy, has no surname. They were the first men buried under a new law which decreed that shipwrecked bodies should be buried at public expense, with rewards for those who found them. The present memorial is a beautifully carved replica of the original.

In the churchyard at Twynning (Gloucs) are two buff-coloured *ceramic* hearts of unbelievable hideousness and unsuitability. They date from early this century, but unfortunately they have failed to weather or attract lichens and can only be left as an example of inappropriate materials. By contrast at Madeley (Shrops) there is a small stone with a ceramic insert; however more important is the loss of the mosaic headstone to Charles Turner who died in 1906, which was in pieces in the vestry; it was presumably made at the local tile works and is quite unique. *Cast iron* is used extensively for churchyard memorials, most often in the form of a small Celtic cross, and nearly every churchyard has one or two. At St Erth (Cnwll) is a whole group of small decorated crosses, many of them to children. Madeley (Shrops), at the heart of the ironfounding industry, has the best collection of cast iron memorials **(71)**. The handsome painted memorial to

72 *Painted cast-iron memorial, Long Melford, Suffolk*

William Baldwin, a monument in every sense of the word to one of our greatest industries, stands enclosed by elegant railings; others were newly painted, including a chest tomb to Rev John Fletcher (d 1785) and his wife; also her descendant, Mary Tooth, who died in 1843, painted in black and white with the puzzling epitaph 'Her Warfare is Accomplished'. A row of cast-iron ledgers records the victims of a pit disaster 'who were killed by the unhooking of the chains on which they were ascending the shaft of the Brickkiln Leasow Crawsfone Pit in this parish at the end of their day's labour on Tuesday the 27th of September 1864'. In the parish records is a Closure Order signed personally by Queen Victoria in 1856 relating to part of the churchyard, as a result of which a pit containing cholera victims is now outside the boundary.

Long Melford (Suffk) has a veritable forest of small cast-iron headstones, as well as a cast-iron bodystone and a handsome painted memorial to Thomas Greer, 1887 (**72**). In the same churchyard and also at Lavenham are a number of cast-iron inserts set into headstones, an unusual and effective combination of materials. The parish of Long Melford not only has its parish bier in use, complete with brass fittings; it has a funeral director in top hat and morning coat to officiate.

73 Elegant railings at Tidcombe, Wilts

In the redundant churchyard of Sutton Veny (Wilts) are two bodystones, and also an ogee-shaped cage over a ledger which is reminiscent of the mediaeval custom of using willow wands to prevent sheep from disturbing new graves (see p.24).

Pedestal tombs in cast iron are unusual, except in local areas where there are foundries; there is a large group at Stourport (Worcs) commemorating the Baldwin family at whose foundry they were made, and a pair at Pontesbury (Shrops). In Wiltshire there is an isolated cast iron headstone at Kingston Langley, and at Beckington (Somset) is the attractive bodystone to Charles Moody, decorated with tulip heads and a crucifix. At Burrington (Herefs) is an unusually early group of cast iron ledgers to the Knight family which were originally in the church. They date from 1619–1754 and most have coats-of-arms in relief. The Knights had an iron foundry in Shropshire.

Railings surrounding churchyard memorials began to appear in the eightteenth century at a time when the population were preoccupied with the fear of bodysnatchers and the desire to leave the deceased undisturbed. Early work carried out by local blacksmiths had a simplicity of design in both wrought and cast iron which can still be found in churchyards today: simple spearhead verticals and rounded urns at the corners. Later they came to represent the Victorian obsession with privacy, with increased intricacy of design as the industrial processes took over. By the end of the nineteenth century they were appearing in catalogues in a wide range of designs. Finally the need for metal during the second world war meant that many were removed.

135

To take just one county, in Wiltshire there are attractive railings with corner finials at Tidcombe and at Oaksey; at Melksham, where they surround a circular monument, the bottom rail has ball feet. At Lacock heavy scrolled railings — the word seems inappropriate — surround the tomb of Rear Admiral Charles Fielding who died in 1837.

At Wylye an elegant eighteenth-century railed enclosure on the boundary has scrolled panels and twisted corner posts with small vase finials in a combination of cast and wrought iron. Local legend has it that a seemingly impoverished man called Popjay who had left the village returned at a later date with all the outward signs of wealth and ordered the monument to be built. He then disappeared without paying for it, never to be seen again. There is no visible tomb within the enclosure.

10 The survey

This study of English Churchyard Memorials has been based on a survey of those memorials listed Grade I and Grade II* by the Royal Commission on the Historical Monuments of England (RCHME).[1] The objectives of the study have been:

- to identify, examine and record those memorials listed by the RCHME as being of importance in terms of antiquity, architectural importance, historical importance or group value
- to establish the present state of repair of those memorials
- to create a positive awareness of the importance of many of our churchyard memorials as part of our architectural, archaeological and social history.

As an indication of the extent of the survey, 254 memorials and 16 churchyard mausolea (Appendix 2) in 140 locations have been visited. Where memorials are listed as a group they have been assessed as a group. Churchyard crosses (Appendix 1) have not all been seen. The condition of the memorials (Appendix 3) is recorded as good, fair or poor on two counts: (a) general condition and stability, (b) the condition of any sculpture and inscription.

The outcome of the survey was as follows:

(a) Although a large proportion of older memorials have sunk to some extent, all but 25 (10%) were in a generally stable condition. Of these only two, Sapperton (Gloucs) and South Brewham (Somset) could be described as critical.

(b) Sculpture and inscriptions have obviously deteriorated over the years, and in most cases must be accepted as normal weathering. In a few exceptional circumstances such as the Knowles tomb at Elmore (Gloucs) where one figure on the north side has all but disappeared, the damaged stonework should be replaced.

Classification
Classification of historic buildings is divided into ancient monuments, listed buildings and conservation areas. For the purposes of this study the category of ancient monuments applies only to early crosses and some hogbacks. A significant proportion of churchyard monuments are classified under listed buildings.

During the research a significant number of errors were discovered in the RCHME Listed Buildings System. Inevitably this has considerably hampered the study, particularly where a simple typing error has inflated a Grade II to a Grade I. It rapidly became obvious that the Listed Buildings System was unreliable and therefore worthless without extensive cross-checking; the author has used her considerable personal knowledge as well as other sources to complete the study.

Listed Buildings regulations
The Planning (Listed Buildings and Conservation Areas) Act 1990 provides specific protection for buildings of special architectural interest. Historic buildings are placed in one of three categories to give an indication of their relative importance.[2] In England the position at present is:

Grade I	9,000	(2%)
Grade II★	18,000	(4%)
Grade II	416,000	(94%)
Total	443,000	

Buildings (including churchyard memorials) can be added to or removed from the statutory lists either by regular re-surveying or by 'spot-listing.' The criteria for listing fall into four categories:

- architectural interest, including the design, decoration and craftmanship in terms of quality, rarity and excellence.
- historic interest, i.e. those which are important as part of the nation's cultural, economic or military history;
- close historical association with nationally important people or events;
- group value, where buildings collectively make up an important group or area.

In addition, age is a consideration: buildings from before 1700 are always listed for historic interest, as are the majority of buildings between 1700 and 1840. After that date so much building took place that the system is more selective, and buildings less than ten years old are not listed.

The listing system was only applied to churchyard memorials in the early 1980s; the majority seem to have been surveyed once and not again. Inevitably there are inconsistencies: many seventeenth-century memorials are sunk or in a state of collapse, their inscriptions eroded and illegible, their sculpture fallen victim to erosion or vandalism. The blurred lines between Grade II and Grade II★ are illustrated by three seventeenth-century early chest tombs at Combe Raleigh and Cotleigh (Devon). The memorials, in Beer stone exhibit unusual and primitive decoration under massive ledgers, yet they are listed Grade II.

Headstones are usually excluded, in spite of their value as examples of folk art and symbolism (see Littledean p.96 and Broadway p.92). There are of course regional variations: it is noticeable that much of the exceptional work in the Cotswolds is listed Grade II, and it is difficult not to feel that many of these would merit a listing of Grade II★ if they were not in the centre of such *richesse* (see Palling memorial p.68).

Diocesan Regulations

Jurisdiction over churchyards resides with the bishop, in whom is vested the responsibility to preserve their aesthetic appeal and character and maintain some control over the erection of inappropriate designs or materials. Any sizeable alterations, levelling of graves or re-siting of memorials cannot be carried out without a faculty. The responsibility for the care and maintenance of the churchyard rests with the Parochial Church Council, who may be found liable for damage or injury caused by unsafe memorials. It is required to be fenced and kept 'in such an orderly and decent manner as becomes consecrated land.'[3] Where a churchyard is closed to burials the responsibility for upkeep may be transferred to the Local Authority.

The diocese has control over what memorials may or may not be erected in the churchyard, and even what inscriptions may be permissible, an area which has become controversial in recent years. In the Diocese of Worcester, for example the permitted maximum dimensions for headstones are:

Height	4' 0" (1200mm)
Width	3' 0" (900mm)
Thickness	6" (150mm)

There is no automatic right to erect a memorial, and strictly speaking every memorial requires a faculty. However in practice the incumbent is authorised to grant permission within certain limits. Inappropriate designs or materials, such as granite or marble, are discouraged, and anyone wishing to erect a memorial outside the limits of the incumbent's authority would have to get a faculty, a process which can be time-consuming and expensive. Fortunately imaginative and individual designs by craftsmen in local stone are encouraged, as a result of which some good modern work is now appearing in our churchyards and cemeteries. Unfortunately in some areas innovative and enlightened modern work finds itself restricted by rigid diocesan regulations, and variations between one diocese and another can seem discriminatory and unfair.

Since 1953 'unseemly' epitaphs have been banned, so that inscriptions in some dioceses are now limited to a factual statement and perhaps a line from the bible. A note in *The Churchyards Handbook* says: 'Inscriptions must be simple and reverent, and may include felicitous quotations from literary sources'.[4]

The churchyard today

Underlying the concerns regarding the care and maintenance of the modern churchyard is of course the fundamental principle of respect for the dead. But in practical terms upkeep and management present something of a dilemma to Parochial Church Councils and parishioners. While the romantic vision may be of leaning, lichen-covered headstones the reality is more likely to be crumbling chest tombs and sinking headstones which bear witness to the ravages of time, weather and neglect. They are costly to repair and if allowed to fall into disrepair can be dangerous; the work involved in repair or conservation is

74 Modern repair to a lyre-ended tomb at Painswick, Gloucs

specialised, time-consuming, and therefore expensive.

So who cares if they fall down? The families whose ancestors they represent are more often than not no longer in the district, and even if they are, there is no enforceable legal action to require them to carry out repairs. Churchyard memorials are not usually at the top of the priority list when the church fabric is crumbling or the organ has woodworm. There seems to be a lack of interest in this particular corner of parish history; a shrugging of shoulders and a feeling that nobody will notice or care if a chest tomb collapses.

The structural repair of chest tombs is specialised work: stone decay is unpredictable, even where stone has been taken from the same quarry at the same time it can differ in weathering properties. Deterioration can also vary according to aspect and exposure. Sometimes all that is required is the replacement of one panel, as has been done so successfully recently at Painswick **(74)**; more often the whole tomb will need to be dismantled, the foundations or vault made good and the tomb reassembled with stainless steel fixing pins and new stone added where necessary. In the diocese of Gloucester a Table Tomb Fund was set up by the late Dame Joan Evans in 1960 as a reflection of her concern for the beautiful and irreplaceable Cotswold monuments. The Diocesan Advisory Committee holds a list of stonemasons whom they recommend for carrying out repairs to churchyard monuments.

A major problem with rescuing sinking headstones before they disappear entirely is that bringing them out can hasten the destruction of the sculpture and inscriptions. Headstones that have been in the ground may still be in mint condition after two or three hundred years; bringing them to the surface and exposing them to a combination of rain and frost begins the process of destruction. The only answer seems to be to leave them partly embedded in the soil and cut a small trench or ditch in front of the stone so that the carving is afforded some protection.

One of the main culprits in the destruction of chest and pedestal tombs is ivy, which if left unattended will rapidly erode the stone and ultimately cause the collapse of the tomb. A beautiful Grade II eighteenth-century chest tomb at Elmore (Gloucs) was recently brought down by ivy; the roots inside the tomb were three inches in diameter. The Living Churchyards Project has agreed that the dense plinth of ivy round the base of a memorial can be sprayed with a herbicide such as Roundup, which will kill the roots. It is of course vital that no chemicals are sprayed on the stone.

In recent years a number of changes have taken place in the modern churchyard. The most noticeable of these is the arrival of small stone cremation plaques which mark the interment of ashes and provide a focal point for the bereaved. In *The Churchyards Handbook* (1988)[5] the editors indicate that previous encouragement of this type of memorial was a mistake, and that 'some churchyards are fast becoming covered with crazy paving'. In some areas Parochial Church Councils have got round this problem by designating a specific area for the scattering of ashes and setting the plaques into a wall or stone block. This has been done effectively at Tealby (Lincs) and St Mary's (Isles of Scilly). At Upper Cam (Gloucs) an area has been set aside with seats and flower beds. On three sides the area for ashes has been created behind a curb and uniform small bronze plaques recording the deceased are fixed to the curb. The effect is ordered but restful, providing a focus in a secluded and sympathetic setting for those who grieve.

There has been much discussion in recent years about so-called 'green' burials. With approximately 200,000 new burials every year and twice that number of cremations, concerns have been raised about the amount of land required for cemeteries, and about the volume of emissions from crematoria. Apart from the waste of good wood, conventional coffins contain laminates and toxic glues which not only pollute the atmosphere but in burials contaminate the soil.

Woodland burials take place on green sites, usually farmland, using bio-degradable coffins and replacing headstones with young trees. The sites are carefully recorded and a plaque may be attached to the tree or buried just beneath the soil. Generally the cost is very much less than that of a conventional funeral. The Natural Death Centre was established in 1991 and reports that there are now 90 sites open with another 40 projected, an indication of the interest created. The Church of England has recently announced its first woodland burial site near Cambridge; coffins will be bio-degradable and trees will mark the burial sites.

One encouraging development in the last few years has been the growth in membership of Family History Societies. Literally thousands of ordinary people have begun the search for their ancestors in parish records and in churchyards, generating an increased interest in churchyard memorials and a considerable skill in deciphering worn inscriptions. In addition the computerisation of records and their availability on microfiche has brought genealogy into the twenty-first century.

Where a church has been taken over by the Churches Conservation Trust (previously The Redundant Churches Fund) the churchyard is not necessarily in their care. However they make every attempt ensure that it continues to be cared for, perhaps by a local naturalist club or by individuals. Many redundant churchyards such as Lassington (Gloucs) and Sutton Veny (Wilts) have a peaceful and evocative atmosphere.

Conclusions

At a time of shrinking church congregations and parish funds, it is clearly neither practicable nor realistic to conserve all churchyard memorials. One of the side-effects of listing is that it becomes easier to raise funds for repairs to listed memorials from sources such as the Lottery Heritage Fund and grant-making trusts. Certainly the higher the grade of listing, the easier it can be. At Standish (Gloucs), for example, which has one memorial listed Grade II★ and a large number listed Grade II, it took considerable time and effort on the part of one parishioner to obtain a Lottery Heritage grant for the repair of the memorials. Painswick is another matter: it is part of a conservation area and has a large number of tourists as well as a sizeable congregation; they are to be congratulated on their 'showpiece' churchyard and particularly their Tomb Trail.

Listing is no guarantee of protection, and the financial constrictions of small parishes mean that when repairs are necessary the churchyard is a low priority. However if the Listed Buildings System is intended to draw attention to those which are deemed to be of importance, it is largely failing to protect many of them, including the vast majority of those listed Grade II. For reasons which include lack of funds, lack of interest and changing social patterns, almost any churchyard will bear witness to leaning, ivy-covered memorials and sinking headstones. This is sadly demonstrated by the condition of the Grade II Anthony memorial, 1707, at Beaconsfield (Bucks), a large pedestal tomb which is falling into its own vault at an angle of 45^0 **(75)**. Work such as this is not being done today: when it has gone it is lost forever; we do not allow other historic buildings to degenerate into crumbling ruins.

In a few exceptional instances such as Elmore (Gloucs) where small parishes do not have the resources or the manpower to maintain listed memorials, the whole churchyard would merit group listing as a conservation area and the responsibility for care and repair of the memorials be shared with the Diocesan Advisory Committee.

Wholesale clearance of memorials is not the answer, especially if solely for the ease of mowing. In rural areas sheep are returning as an acceptable solution to the problems of mowing and can be kept off sensitive areas by plastic netting. The Living Churchyard and Cemeterys Project has had a considerable impact on the management of churchyards for wildlife, and by careful planning are able to reduce some of the work involved.

How long a grave marker should stand is open to debate; even when memories and inscriptions have faded it still identifies the site of interment. A large number of churchyard memorials are works of art in their own right, and as such are worthy of preservation. Some of the memorials are as much part of our architectural heritage as the church itself and the buildings that surround it.

75 *Collapsing listed tomb at Beaconsfield*

The churchyard is an ancient, consecrated and spiritual place. The dead who lie beneath that soil are a part of the village history; their memorials and the inscriptions on them form part of the social, architectural and genealogical history of the community and as such must at least be recorded, and where possible preserved for future generations to appreciate and enjoy.

Footnotes

Chapter 1
1 *Of Graves and Epitaphs*

Chapter 2
1 Bede's *Ecclesiastical History* Book I Chapter XXIII
2 Ibid. Book III Chapter XXVI
3 Bizley Alice C, *The Slate Figures of Cornwall*
4. Cook G H, *The Mediaeval Parish Church*
5 Lindley Kenneth, *Of Graves and Epitaphs*

Chapter 3
1 For churchyard crosses listed Grade I and Grade II★ see appendix 1

Chapter 4
1 Baldwin Browne. Prof G, *Antiquaries Journal* II 1931
2 Bede's *Ecclesiastical History* Book III Chapter XXVIII
3 Pevsner N, *Buildings of England. Wiltshire*
4 Burgess F, *English Churchyard Memorials* 1963
5 Blomefield F, *An Essay Towards a Topographical History of Norfolk* 1739 Vol. V
6 Ibid Vol VIII
7 Laing L & J, *Mediaeval Britain*. Herbert Press 1998
8 Smith Phillippa J F, *A Short History of Dacre Parish Church*

Chapter 5
1 Weever J, *A Discourse on Funerall Monuments.* London 1631
2 Burgess F B, *English Churchyard Memorials.* Chapter 2
3 Clifton Taylor Alec, *English Parishes Churches as works of Art.* Batsford 1974 Chapter 3
4 Dickinson Bickford H C, Church leaflet
5 Burgess F, *English Churchyard Memorials.* Chapter 2
6 Summerson J, *The Pelican History of Art.* Chapter 10
7 Elliot W R, *Chest tombs and Teacaddies by Cotswold & Severn*

Chapter 6
1 Rudder Samuel, *History of Gloucestershire* 1779
2 Pevsner N, *Buildings of England Series*
3 Bowdler Roger, *Churchscape no 17* (Council for the Care of Churches)

Chapter 7
1 Innes Hart, 'Rude Forefathers', *Architectural Review* 1939
2 National Art Library, Victoria and Albert Museum, London
3 Chinnery V, *Oak Furniture* 1979

Chapter 8
1 'The Cornish Engraver', Brown Eric & Everard Enid, *Architectural Review* Vol 95. 1944
2 *The Art of Remembering*, ed Frazer Harriet & Ostreicher Christine. Carcanet Press 1998
3 Weever J, A Discourse of Funerall Monuments. London 1961
4 Bigland R, Historical Monuments and Genealogical Collections

Chapter 9
1 Burgess F, *English Churchyard Memorials*

Chapter 10
1 Note: There have inevitably been errors in the transcribing of thousands of records on to the RCHME Listed Buildings Database. The author would be glad to know of any such errors in the text
2 *Planning Policy Guidance* Sept 1994
3 *The Churchyards Handbook* Chapter 5
4 Ibid Appendix 1
5 Ibid Chapter 1

Glossary

Acanthus — leaf used in classical ornament

Acroteria — pedestal or decorative finial used in classical building

Arca — classical form of sarcophagus, often supported on lions' feet

Bale tomb — chest tomb surmounted by a semi-cylindrical or grooved capping stone with scalloped ends

Bodystone — stone, rounded or oval in cross-section, covering a grave

Cartouche — decorative panel with scrolled surround

Caryatid — female figure supporting a column

Chamfer — a cut-away area of stone where two surfaces meet

Chest tomb — stone box placed over a burial site

Chi-Rho — first two letters of Christ's name in Greek, used as a sacred monogram

Church Ales — festivities held in mediaeval churchyards to raise money

Cist — a box-like tomb-chamber made of stone slabs

Classical — style of architecture based on Greek and Roman designs

Coffin slab — coffin-shaped lid to coffin

Coffin stone — raised block of stone under lych gate on which coffin was rested

Columbarium — structure similar to a dovecote for storing coffins or urns

Console — s-shaped bracket supporting horizontal or vertical surface

Coped stone — ridged or gabled memorial stone

Discoid — wood or stone round grave marker

Dole table — slab or tomb in the churchyard from which bread and alms were distributed to the poor

Epitaph — comment or rhyme on tombstones describing the character or fate of the deceased

Finial — ornamental knob on top of memorial

Footstone — small stone marking the foot of the grave

Gadroon — decorative moulding consisting of a series of convex flutes

Gothic Revival — early nineteenth-century revival of Gothic style

Graveboard — inscribed board along length of grave

Grotesque — caricature, usually in stone, on exterior of church

Guilloche — classical ornament of interweaving circular bands

Headstone — shaped stone at the head of the grave, usually inscribed

Hogback — horizontal memorial of Scandinavian origin found in the North

Latten — copper alloy used for memorial plates

Ledger — large, flat stone covering a grave

Lozenge — diamond-shaped decoration

Lychgate — covered entrance to the churchyard

Lyre end — the characteristic shape of the end and console on the Cotswold chest tomb

Mausoleum — a family burial house

Obelisk — tapering shaft of stone used as a monument

Ogham — celtic script found on the edges of upright stones

Patera — circular ornament or medallion, often in association with fluting

Pedestal tomb — a memorial that is higher than it is wide

Pilaster — flat column built against a vertical surface

Quatrefoil — ornamental four-lobed decoration of Gothic design

Rococo — latest phase of Baroque architecture

Rosette — patera (qv) with floral embellishment

Sarcophagus — ornate stone coffin or coffin-like memorial

Sheela-na-gig — carvings representing fertility figures

Spandrel — triangular space between an arch and its rectangular frame

Standing stone — prehistoric stone of pagan origin

Stela — upright carved gravestone, usually Roman

Strigillation — curved pattern of s-shaped flutes

Table tomb — inscribed slab or ledger raised on supporting columns

Tympanum — space between the lintel of a doorway and the arch above, often decorated

Volute — scroll or coil of the Ionic capital

Weepers — mourning figures carved on memorials

Appendices

Appendix 1:   Crosses and hogbacks listed Grade I and Grade II★

PLACE	COUNTY	GRADE	TYPE
Albrighton	Shrops	II★	cross
Alderbury/ Cardeston	Shrops	II★	cross
Alstonefield	Staffs	II★	base of cross shaft
Ampney Crucis	Gloucs	I	cross
Arthuret	Cumbria	II★	cross
Asgarby/Howell	Lincs	II★	cross
Badger	Shrops	II★	cross
Badgworth	Somerset	II★	cross
Bakewell	Derbys	I	cross
Bewcastle	Cumbria	I A/Mon	cross shaft
Bicknoller	Devon	II★	cross
Binbrook	Lincs	II★	cross
Bitterley	Shrops	I A/Mon	cross
Blanchland	Northumb	I	cross
Bradford Abbas	Dorset	I	cross
Broadway	Somerset	II★	cross
Broomfield	Somerset	II★	cross
Burtholme	Cumbria	I	cross base
Butcombe	Somerset	II★	cross
Cardinham	Cornwall	II★	cross
Caynham	Shrops	II★	cross
Charlton Kings	Gloucs	II★	cross
Charlton on Otmoor	Oxon	II★	cross
Chewton Mendip	Somerset	I	cross
Closworth	Somerset	II★	cross
Coddington	H&W	II★	cross
Colwall	H&W	II★	cross
Compton Bishop	Somerset	II★	cross
Cricklade	Wilts	I	cross
Crowcombe	Somerset	II★	cross
Culbone	Somerset	II★	cross
Darlington	Durham	A/Mon	hogback inside
Dodington	Somerset	II★	remains of cross
Donington	Shrops	II★	cross
Dorchester	Oxon	I	cross
Drayton	Somerset	II★	cross
E Quantoxhead	Somerset	II★	cross
Enmore	Somerset	II★	cross
Eyam	Derbys	I	cross
Gosforth	Cumbria	I A/Mon	cross
Great Bedwyn	Wilts	II★	cross
Hampton Bishop	H&W	II★	cross
Heathfield	Somerset	II★	cross
Higham Ferrars	NHants	I	cross
Hoby/Rotherby	Leics	II★	cross
Holford	Somerset	II★	cross
Ightfield	Shrops	A/ Mon	cross

Ilam	Staffs	I	cross shaft
Ilam	Staffs	I	cross shaft
Inglesham	Wilts	II★	cross
Lancaster	Lancs	I A/Mon	hogback
Langford	Oxon	II★	cross
Lanivet	Cornwall	II★ A/Mon	hogback & cross
Lanteglos	Cornwall	II★	cross
Luccombe	Somerset	II★	remains of cross
Madley	H&W	II★	cross
Masham	Yorks	I	cross
Maxstoke	Warcs	II★	cross
Mordiford	H&W	II★	cross
North Curry	H&W	II★	cross
North Hinksey	Oxon	II★	cross
North Petherton	Somerset	II★	remains of cross
Nynehead	Somerset	II★	remains of cross
Old Cleeve	Somerset	II★	cross
Penrith	Cumbria	I A/Mon	hogback & cross
Preston Plucknett	Somerset	II★	cross
Putley	H&W	II★	cross
Rampisham	Dorset	II★	cross
Ratley & upton	Warcs	II★	cross
Raunds	NHants	II★	cross
Rocester	Staffs	II★	cross
Rockcliffe	Cumbria	I	cross
Ross-on-Wye	H&W	II★	cross
Rudston	Yorks	I A/Mon	monolith
Ruishton	Somerset	II★	cross
Saltash	Cornwall	II★	cross
Sandford	Devon	II★	cross
Selworthy	Somerset	II★	remains of cross
Shelsley Beauchamp	H&W	II★	cross
Shrawley	H&W	II★	cross base
Somerton	Oxon	I	cross
Spaxton	Somerset	I	cross
St Enodoc	Cornwall	I	cross
St Tudy	Cornwall	I	hogback in porch
Stoughton	Leics	II★	cross
Stowford	Devon	II★	monolith
Stratton	Dorset	II★	cross
Stringston	Somerset	II★	cross
Thurleigh	Beds	II★	cross
Tong	Shrops ·	II★	cross
Tortworth	Somerset	II★	cross
Tyberton	H&W	I	cross
Upper Weare	Somerset	II★	cross
W Quantoxhead	Somerset	II★	remains of cross
Walcot	Lincs	I	cross
Walterastone	H&W	II★	cross
Waterperry/Thomley	Oxon	I	cross
Wedmore	Somerset	II★	cross
Wellington	H&W	II★	base & shaft
West Pennard	Somerset	I	cross
Whatley	Somerset	II★	cross
Whitchurch	H & W	II★	cross
Whitchurch	H&W	II★	cross
Williton	Somerset	II★	remains of cross
Wooton Courtenay	Somerset	II★	remains of cross
Yarnton	Oxon	II★	base & shaft
Yealmpton	Devon	II★	monolith

Appendix 2:   Mausolea listed Grade I and Grade II★

PLACE	COUNTY	DATE	GRADE	DETAILS
Barnes	London	1890	II★	Burton mausoleum
Bicton Park	Devon	1834	I	Rolle family/Pugin
Brightling	Sussex	1810	II★	'Mad Jack' Fuller/Sir Robert Smirke
Buckminster	Leics	Victorian	II★	Dysart family
Claverton	Somerset	1764	II★	Ralph Allen/Robert Parsons
Englefield Green	Surrey	1860	II★	Fitzroy family/E B Lamb
Farningham	Kent	1778	II★	Thomas Nash/Nash
Fawley	Bucks	1750	II★	Freeman/John Freeman
Little Ouseburn	Yorks	1760	II★	Henry Thompson/Thompson
Morley	Derbys	1897	II★	Bateman family/G F Bodley
Ombersley	H & W	late 13C	II★	Sandys family
Shotley	Northumb	1752	I	Hopper family/Hopper
Stone	Staffs	c 1760, undated	II★	Jervis family/Robinson
Thurnham	Lancs	1830	II★	Gillow mausoleum
Wargrave	Berks	1906	II★	Hannen family/Lutyens
West Wycombe	Bucks	1763-4	I	Dashwood family/John Bastard
Woodford	London	1797	II★	Raikes family

Appendix 3: Memorials listed Grade I and Grade II*

PLACE	COUNTY	TYPE	GRADE	DETAILS	MATERIALS	CONDITION Memorial	sculpture
Astbury	Cheshire	monument	II*	Brereton 13C	yellow sandstone	good	fair
Barnard Castle	Durham	chest tomb	II*	Hopper 1725	sandstone	good	good
Beaconsfield	Bucks	chest tomb	II*	Waller 1687	marble/stone/railings	good	fair
Bibury	Gloucs	chest tomb etc (6)	II*	17/18C	limestone	good	fair
Alderley	Gloucs	chest tomb	II*	Stanton 1589	limestone	fair	good
Bishops Cannings	Wilts	chest tomb	II*	15C	limestone	good	good
Bourton/Water	Gloucs	chest tomb	II*	Jordan 1774	limestone	good	good
Bovey Tracey (1)	Devon	chest tomb	II*	Forbes 1655	granite ashlar	good	fair
Bovey Tracey (2)	Devon	chest tomb	II*	1678	granite	good	good
Boxwell	Gloucs	chest tomb (3)	II*	17/18C	limestone	good	fair
Broadwell	Gloucs	chest tomb (6+1)	II* + I	Chadwell 17C	limestone	good	good
Broadwoodwidger	Devon	headstone	II*	signed, 1789	slate	good	good
Broomfield	Somerset	chest tomb	II*	Crosse 1653	stone	good	good
Brympton d'Evercy	Somerset	chest tomb etc	II*	16/17C	Ham Hill stone/lias	good	good
Buckland	Gloucs	chest tomb	II*	15C	stone	good	good
Burford	Oxon	chest tomb	II*	Aston 1698	limestone	good	fair
Burton Lazars	Leics	chest tomb	II*	Squires 1781	stone/railings	good	fair
Caenby	Lincs	gravestone	II*	13C	ashlar	good	fair
Castle Cary	Somerset	chest tomb	II*	Cosenes 1590	Doulting	good	good
Chippenham	Wilts	monument	II*	Ricardo 1823	ashlar & marble	good	good
Cirencester	Gloucs	monument	II*	Captain Day 1790	limestone	good	good
Closworth	Somerset	chest tomb	II*	Collins 1570,1609	Ham Hill, lead inserts	good	good
Compton Abdale	Gloucs	chest tomb	II*	14C	limestone	good	poor
Cowley	Gloucs	chest tomb	II*	Briggs 1709	limestone	good	poor
Cricklade	Wilts	chest tomb	II*	15-16C	limestone	good	good
Cucklington	Somerset	chest tomb	II*	Thorne 1617	Doulting	poor	good
Dacre	Cumbria	bears (4)	II*	mediaeval	red sandstone	good	good
Daglingworth	Gloucs	chest tomb	II*	Heines 1683	limestone	good	good
Dymock	Gloucs	chest tomb	II*	Smith 1746, dole	stone	good	good
East Hagbourne	Oxon	chest tomb	II*	Phillips 1736	marble, stone, railings	good	good
Easton Grey	Wilts	chest tomb	II*	Adye 1731	limestone	good	good

Elkstone	Gloucs	chest tomb	II*	Poole 1692	limestone	good	good
Elmore	Gloucs	chest tomb	II*	Knowles 1707	limestone	good	fair
Epworth	Lincs	chest tomb	I	Wesley 1735	ashlar	good	good
Fairford (1)	Gloucs	chest tombs (3)	II*	Morgan 1728	limestone	good	fair
Fairford (2)	Gloucs	chest tomb	II*	Strong 1662	limestone	good	good
Fairford (3)	Gloucs	chest tomb	II*	15C	limestone	good	good
Felling	Tyne & Wear	chest tomb	II*	Haddon 1717	sandstone	good	good
Foulsham	Norfolk	chest tomb	II*	Colles 1505	stone	good	fair
Fulbrook	Oxon	chest tomb	II*	15C	limestone	good	good
Godmanstone	Dorset	chest omb	II*	Pitman 1717	stone	good	fair
Grasmere	Cumbria	headstones	II*	Wordsworth	stone	good	good
Great Moulton	Norfolk	chest tomb	II*	15C	slate	good	poor
Hackthorn (1)	Lincs	headstone	I	10C	stone	good	good
Hackthorn (2)	Lincs	gravestone	I	10C	ashlar	fair	poor
Hardwicke	Gloucs	chest tomb	II*	Smith 1675	ashlar	good	good
Haresfield (1)	Gloucs	chest tomb (3)	II*	early 18C	limestone	good	good
Haresfield (2)	Gloucs	chest tomb (3)	II*	early 18C	limestone	good	good
Haresfield (3)	Gloucs	chest tomb (2)	II*	late 17C	limestone	good	good
Haresfield (4)	Gloucs	chest tomb (5) HS (2)	II*	mid/late 18C	limestone	good	fair
Hartpury	Gloucs	chest tomb	II*	Sloper 1703	ashlar	good	poor
Hewelsfield	Gloucs	chest tomb	II*	late 17C	sandstone	fair	fair
Heysham	Lancs	graves (6)	I	pre-Conquest		good	n/a
Heysham	Lancs	graves (2)	I	pre-Conquest		good	n/a
Horsley (1)	Gloucs	chest tomb	II*	18C	limestone	good	good
Horsley (2)	Gloucs	mons (2)	II*	18C	limestone	fair	fair
Howick Hall	Northumb	grave stones (4)	II*	13C	sandstone	good	fair
Ilam	Staffs	grave stone	II*	13C	stone	good	good
Isel	Cumbria	chest tomb	II*	15C	red sandstone	good	fair
Kilmersdon (1)	Somerset	monument	II*	Jolliffe 1918	stone	good	good
Kilmersdon (2)	Somerset	chest tomb (4) HS (3)	II*	17C	stone/slate	good	good
Kilve	Somerset	chest tomb	II*	Pollard 17C	Ham stone	good	fair
Kingston Seymour	Somerset	chest tomb	II*	15/16C	stone	fair	fair
Kington St Michael	Wilts	chest tomb (9)	II*	18C	ashlar	fair	fair
Lambeth	London	chest tomb (3)	II*	Bligh, Tradescant, Sealy	Coade stone	good	good
Lew Trenchard	Devon	chest tomb	II*	Wood, 1623	granite	good	fair
Leyland	Lancs	chest tomb	II*	Walker 1588	stone	good	fair

Long Ashton	Somerset	chest tomb (7)	II*	Whiting etc 17C	limestone	good	good
Longney	Gloucs	chest tomb	II*	Pack 1695	limestone	fair	good
Loversall	Yorks	chest tomb	II*	14C	magnesian limestone	good	good
Lovington	Somerset	chest tomb	II*	Hole 1623	Doulting	good	fair
Low Dinsdale	Durham	coffin and lid	II*	stone	stone	good	good
Lower Wraxall	Dorset	chest tomb	II*	Cattistock 1728	stone	good	good
Lydney (1)	Gloucs	chest tomb	II*	Berrow 1632	Forest stone	fair	fair
Lydney (2)	Gloucs	chest tomb	II*	North 1633	Forest stone	fair	poor
Lydney (3)	Gloucs	chest tomb	II*	17C	Forest stone	fair	good
Mickle Trafford	Cheshire	chest tomb etc	II*	Hurleston 1670	sandstone	good	good
Milborne Port	Somerset	chest tomb	II*	Prankerd 1609	Ham Hill stone	good	good
Mileham	Norfolk	cross on chest tomb	II*	15C	ashlar	good	good
Minchinhampton	Gloucs	pedestal	II*	18C	limestone	good	fair
Morland	Cumbria	chest tomb	II*	15C	sandstone	fair	poor
Morwenstow	Cornwall	chest tomb	II*	Manning 1601	granite	good	good
Necton	Norfolk	chest tomb + effigy	II*	14C	limestone	good	good
Netherbury	Dorset	chest tomb (7)	II*	18C	limestone	good	good
Newby	Cumbria	ledger	II*	Lawson 1691	stone	good	good
North Nibley	Gloucs	chest tomb	II*	18C	limestone	fair	poor
Northleach	Gloucs	chest tomb	II*	17C	limestone	good	good
Oddington	Gloucs	chest tomb	II*	Parsons 1695	limestone	good	good
Painswick (1)	Gloucs	chst tmb (2),ldgr, HS	II*	Gardiner 1793 etc	limestone	good	fair
Painswick (2)	Gloucs	chest tombs etc	II*	Packer etc 16C	limestone	good	good
Painswick (3)	Gloucs	chest tombs etc	II*	Smith 1727 etc	limestone	good	good
Painswick(4)	Gloucs	chst tmb,3 headstones	II*	1623	limestone	good	fair
Painswick (5)	Gloucs	monument	II*	John Bryan 1787	limestone	good	good
Pitchcombe	Gloucs	chest tomb (9)	II*	18C	limestone	fair	fair
Podimore	Somerset	chest tomb	II*	16/17th C insc	Ham stone	good	good
Prestbury	Gloucs	chest tomb	II*	Kemmet 1716	limestone	good	good
Richmond	London	chest tomb (2)	II*	Gainsborough, Zoffany	stone	good	good
Rodney Stoke	Somerset	chest tomb	II*	15C	stone	good	fair
Sapperton	Gloucs	chest tomb	II*	Baldwin 1677	limestone	poor	fair
Sheen	Staffs	chest tomb	II*	Critchlow 1853	stone/railings	good	good
Shipton/Wychwood	Oxon	chest tomb	II*	Morgan 1727	limestone	good	good
Slimbridge (1)	Gloucs	chest tomb	II*	18C	limestone	good	good
Slimbridge (2)	Gloucs	chest tomb	II*	18C	limestone	good	good

Place	County	Type	Reference	Grade	Material	Condition 1	Condition 2
South Brewham	Somerset	chest tomb	Manning 1618	II*	Doulting Stone	poor	poor
St Briavels	Gloucs	chest tomb	Gough 1691	II*	Forest stone	poor	poor
St Briavels	Gloucs	chest tomb	Butler 1688	II*	Forest stone	good	fair
Standish	Gloucs	chest tomb	Niblett 1676	II*	limestone	good	good
Steeple Ashton	Wilts	chest tomb (2)	18C	II*	limestone	fair	fair
Stinchcombe (1)	Gloucs	chest tomb	Hicks 1739	II*	limestone	good	good
Stinchcombe (2)	Gloucs	chest tomb	Hicks 1728	II*	limestone	good	good
Stinchcombe (3)	Gloucs	chest tomb	18C	II*	limestone	good	good
Stinchcombe (4)	Gloucs	chest tomb (2)	Bendall 1765	II*	limestone	good	good
Stoke-sub-Hamdon	Somerset	chest tomb	Gndry 1659, Jnsn 1707	II*	Ham stone	fair	good
Stone	Staffs	chest tomb	Crompton 1603	II*	stone	good	fair
Stonehouse	Gloucs	chest tomb (12)	17/18C group	II*	limestone	fair	good
Stringston (1)	Somerset	chest tomb	Prior 1618	II*	sandstone/blue lias	good	good
Stringston (2)	Somerset	chest tomb	Garett 1618	II*	sandstone/blue lias	good	good
Sutton Courtenay	Oxon	chest tomb	15C	II*	limestone	fair	poor
Swithland	Leics	chest tomb	Hind 1745	II*	slate, brass, railings	good	good
Tetbury (1)	Gloucs	monument	18C	II*	limestone	fair	poor
Tetbury (2)	Gloucs	pedestal tomb	18C	II*	limestone	good	fair
Tetbury (3)	Gloucs	chest tomb	18C	II*	limestone	good	good
Tolpuddle	Dorset	headstone	Hammett 1891	II*	limestone	good	good
Tredington	Gloucs	chest tomb	17C	II*	limestone	fair	poor
Uley (1)	Gloucs	chest tomb	18C	II*	limestone	good	good
Uley (2)	Gloucs	pedestal tomb	19C	II*	sandstone	good	good
Uley (3)	Gloucs	chest tomb	18C	II*	limestone	good	good
Upper Cam (grp 1)	Gloucs	chest tomb (12)	Phillimore 17/18C	II*	limestone	good	good
Upper Cam (grp 2)	Gloucs	chest tomb (7)	Trotman etc 17/18C	II*	limestone	poor	poor
Upton St Leonards	Gloucs	chest tomb	Ockold 1689	II*	limestone	good	good
Upton St Leonards	Gloucs	chest tomb	Ockold 1657	II*	limestone	good	good
West Monkton	Somerset	chest tomb	17C	II*	Ham stone	good	fair
Windrush (1)	Gloucs	chest tomb, headstone	Newman 1713	II*	limestone	good	good
Windrush (2)	Gloucs	chest tomb, headstone	Trinder 1677	II*	limestone	good	good
Winson	Gloucs	chest tomb (9)	Howse 18/19C	II*	limestone	good	good
Wntrbrne Steepleton	Dorset	chest tomb	18C	II*	stone	good	fair
Woolaston (1)	Gloucs	chest tomb	Smart 17C	II*	Forest stone	good	good
Woolaston (2)	Gloucs	chest tomb	Smart 1666	II*	Forest stone	good	good
Woolaston (3)	Gloucs	chest tomb	Woodrofe 1665	II*	Forest stone	good	good

Select bibliography

Bailey, Brian *Churchyards of England and Wales* Robert Hale 1987

Bede's *Ecclesiastical History* Dent 1910

Bettey, Prof J H. *Church and Parish* Batsford 1987

Bigland, Ralph *Historical Monuments and Genealogical Collections* Bristol & Gloucestershire Archaeological Society (no date)

Bizley, Alice *The Slate Figures of Cornwall* 1965

Brooks, C *Mortal Remains* Wheaton Publishers 1989

Brown, Eric & Everard Enid *The Cornish Engraver* Architectural Review Vol 95.

Burgess, Frederick *English Churchyard Memorials* Lutterworth Press 1963

Burman, Peter & Stapleton, Rev Henry *The Churchyards Handbook* Church House Publishing 1988

Child, Mark *Discovering Churchyards* Shire Publications 1989

Chinnery *Oak Furniture* Antique Collectors' Club 1979

Clifton-Taylor, Alec and Ireson A S *English Stone Building* Gollancz 1983

Colvin, Howard *Architecture and the After-Life* Yale University Press 1991

Cook, G H *The Modern Parish Church* Phoenix House, London. 1954

Churches Conservation Trust *Churches in Retirement* HMSO 1990

Cox, Margaret (Ed) *Grave Concerns* Council for British Archaeology 1998

Crossley, Harold *Lettering in Stone* Self Publishing Assn 1991

Elliott, W R *Chest tombs and Teacaddies by Cotswold and Severn* Bristol & Gloucs Archaeological Society Vol 95

Frazer, Harriet and Oestreicher, Christine *The Art of Remembering*. Carcanet 1998

Hart, Innes *Rude Forefathers* Architectural Review November 1939

Hunter, Doreen & Willsher, Betty *Guide to Some Remarkable 18th Century Gravestones* Canongate 1978

Lang, James *Anglo-Saxon Sculpture* Shire Publications 1988

Lindley, Kenneth *Of Graves and Epitaphs*. Hutchinson 1963

Litten, Julian *The English Way of Death* Robert Hale 1991

Llewellyn, Nigel *The Art of Death* Reaktion Book 1991

Rudder, Samuel *History of Gloucestershire* 1779

Pevsner, Nikolaus *Buildings of England* Series

Summerson, John *Architecture in Britain 1530-1830*. Pelican History of Art 1953

Weaver, Lawrence *Memorials and Monuments* Country Life 1915

Weever, J A. *A Discourse on Funerall Monuments*. London 1631

Wright, Geoffrey *Discovering Epitaphs* Shire Publications 1987

Useful addresses

Memorials by Artists. Snape Priory, Saxmundham, Suffolk IP17 1SA. Tel: 01728 688934

The Living Churchyard and Cemetery Project, The Arthur Rank Centre, Stoneleigh Park, Warwickshire CV8 2LZ. Tel: 10203 696969

Royal Commission on the Historical Monuments of England, Kemble Drive, Swindon SN2 2GZ. Tel: 01793 414600

The Natural Death Centre, 20 Heber raod, London NW2 6AA. Tel:0181 208 2853 (for 'green' burials.)

The Federation of Family History Societies, The Benson Room, Birmingham and Midland Institute, Margaret Street, Birmingham B3 3BS

The Council for the Care of Churches, Fielden House, Little College Street, London SW1P 3SH Tel: 0171 222 3793

Mausolea and Monuments Trust c/o The Georgian Group, 6 Fitzroy Square, London W1P 6DX

Index

SUBJECT INDEX

(bold type indicates illustrations)